Winston Churchill

Winston Churchill

SOLDIER AND POLITICIAN

TRISTAN BOYER BINNS

FRANKLIN WATTS
A Division of Scholastic Inc.
New York Toronto London Auckland Sydney
Mexico City New Delhi Hong Kong
Danbury, Connecticut

To Gethin and Clary for their endless enthusiasm,
and to Kate for giving me time to think.

The Author would like to thank the following sources for permission to reproduce copyright material:

Throughout: Quotations from Sir Winston Churchill reproduced with permission of Curtis Brown, Ltd., London on behalf of The Estate of Sir Winston Churchill, Copyright Sir Winston Churchill; quotations from Parliamentary speeches in chapters three, seven, and ten from Hansard, reproduced with the permission of Her Majesty's Stationery Office; quotations from Lady Clementine Churchill in chapters seven, eight, and ten reproduced with permission of Curtis Brown, Ltd., London on behalf of The Estate of Lady Clementine Churchill, Copyright Lady Soames

Chapter Three: extract from The Natal Witness reproduced with permission of The Natal Witness; extract from *The Diary of Beatrice Webb* edited by N. and J. MacKenzie reproduced with permission of Time Warner Books UK

Chapter Five: extract from Churchill by permission of A. P. Watt on behalf of Sir Martin Gilbert

Chapter Seven: extract reproduced with permission of Curtis Brown, Ltd., Edinburgh on behalf of Ben Pimlott, copyright Ben Pimlott

Chapter Eight: extract reproduced with permission of Curtis Brown, Ltd., London on behalf of The Masters, Fellows and Scholars of Churchill College Cambridge, copyright The Masters, Fellows and Scholars of Churchill College Cambridge; extract reproduced with permission of Curtis Brown, Ltd., London on behalf of Lady Soames DBE, copyright Mary Soames; extract from Harold Nicholson's *Diaries and Letters 1939-45* with permission of HarperCollins Publishers Ltd., © 1945 Harold Nicholson

Chapter Nine: extract from WINSTON CHURCHILL: A BRIEF LIFE by Piers Brendon published by Pimlico. Used by permission of The Random House Group Limited.

Chapter Ten: extract from Clement Attlee speech reproduced with permission of Lord Attlee; extract reproduced with permission of Curtis Brown, Ltd., London on behalf of the estate of Lady Audley, copyright Mary Soames

Chapter Eleven: The Public Papers of the President: John F. Kennedy

Photographs are copyright to their original source and all rights are reserved. Copyright and credits for individual photographs can be found on page 128.

Library of Congress Cataloging-in-Publication Data

Binns, Tristan Boyer, 1968–
  Winston Churchill : soldier and politician / Tristan Boyer Binns.
    p. cm. — (Great life stories)
  Includes bibliographical references and index.
  ISBN 0-531-12361-8
  1. Churchill, Winston, Sir, 1874–1965—Juvenile literature. 2. Great Britain—Politics and government—20th century—Juvenile literature. 3. Prime ministers—Great Britain—Biography—Juvenile literature. 4. World War, 1939–1945—Great Britain-Juvenile literature. I. Title. II. Series.

DA566.9.C5B535 2004
941.084'092-dc22   2004002946

Contents

Winston Churchill made a dramatic entrance into this world. He was born two months early at his grandfather's palace. Here, a two-year-old Winston poses with his mother, Jenny.

ONE

The Early Years

Winston Leonard Spencer Churchill was born on November 30, 1874, at the grand palace of his grandfather, the 7th Duke of Marlborough, near Oxford, in England. While pregnant, his mother fell while out walking. Soon after she went into labor. She was taken to a small bedroom that was mostly used by guests to rest in during parties, and Winston was born there two months early. Winston's parents were so surprised by his arrival that they had no clothes to dress him in!

Winston Churchill became known as a man who could do many things well. He was a politician, a writer, a painter, and even a bricklayer. He was famous for the way he could quickly understand any complex situation and then decide what needed to be done to fix it. He had great energy and charm and knew how to get people to work together. He had a knack for saying what people needed to hear to help them find strength to keep fighting when they were worn out. He was known for sticking to his principles and not being swayed by the lure of personal or political gains. If he thought something was right, he fought for it. If he thought it was wrong, he risked his career to say so.

Winston held many positions in the British government before becoming prime minister twice. The prime minister leads Britain's government much like a U.S. president, though the king or queen is the head of state. Winston was prime minister during World War II, perhaps the most awful and triumphant time ever for both Britain and the United States. He is still remembered today as the man who held Britain together during those difficult years. In fact, in 2002, the British public voted him the greatest Briton of all time.

Winston was part of an aristocratic, upper-class family. His ancestors were involved in the power struggles, politics, and wars that built the British Empire. Some worked closely with England's kings and queens.

Britain's Class System

When Winston Churchill was born, there were strong divisions between people of different social classes in Britain. Upper-class people were usually rich and got their money from their families. They had servants to do household work. They ate well and were educated. Those who did work had safe jobs, such as banking or politics, and owned large amounts of land that they rented to others. Working-class people were poorer and seldom earned enough money to become rich. They often received little education and no health care, and worked under dangerous conditions. It was very difficult to move out of the class into which you were born.

The man who brought the family fame was John Churchill. He won important military battles at the end of the 1600s. Queen Anne gave him a title, the Duke of Marlborough, as a reward. She also gave him Blenheim Palace in 1704, the huge mansion in beautiful parkland grounds where Winston was born. Winston's grandfather, the 7th Duke of Marlborough, was viceroy of Ireland for a few years and represented the British crown in Ireland. Winston's father, Lord Randolph Churchill, had an older brother named Blandford. Because the palace was only passed down to the eldest son, Lord Randolph never owned it. However, his family often visited it.

Lord Randolph Churchill was a member of Parliament, or M.P. He helped govern Britain. Winston's mother was American. Her name was Jennie Jerome, and she grew up in New York City and in Paris. Her father, Leonard Jerome, was a businessman and a great supporter of horse

Lord and Lady Randolph Churchill married soon after their first meeting and began their family quickly.

As a child, Winston was energetic and imaginative, which often got him into trouble at home and school.

racing. He was briefly a part owner of *The New York Times.* Jennie and Randolph met in August 1873 and decided to marry only three days later. They had only been married for seven and a half months when their son Winston was born. Jennie was twenty and Randolph was twenty-five years old.

FAMILY LIFE

About a month after Winston was born, his parents hired Elizabeth Everest to be his nurse. It was common in families such as the Churchills for the children to be looked after by a nurse instead of their parents. Most of Winston's early days were spent with Elizabeth Everest. Later, he also had tutors who taught him reading and math. He wrote, "Mrs. Everest it was who looked after me and tended all my wants. It was to her I poured out my many troubles." Winston called Mrs. Everest "Woomany" or "Woom." Winston's brother Jack was born in 1880. Mrs. Everest looked after both boys.

Winston was thought to be a difficult boy by his parents and some other adults. However, some of his relatives and Mrs. Everest found him delightful. Many of the adults he spent time with had a hard time keeping up with his energy and imagination. He was never content to stay still or to behave. He was always getting into trouble, inventing new ways to do things, and trying to take control of situations. His teachers said he was not to be trusted, didn't know how to work hard and apply himself, and was very naughty. Winston himself admitted that he was very stubborn.

For most of his childhood, Winston's parents had busy social lives. His parents were often away, leaving him and his brother Jack with Mrs. Everest. They stayed in London or traveled to other places. They were often away from each other as well, going to different places.

Winston didn't spend a great deal of time with his parents. He wrote about his mother, "She shone for me like the Evening Star. I loved her dearly—but at a distance." His father was even more distant. He saw little of Lord Randolph. When they were in contact, his father often disapproved of Winston's actions. Many of his letters told Winston what he had done wrong.

Victorian Britain

In 1874, the world was a very different place. There were steam engines, but they only powered some ships and trains. Most people got around by foot or on horses. Most houses had no running water or indoor toilets. There was no electricity to help with chores or to make light. People used candles and lamps to light dark rooms. There was no television, telephone, or recorded music. People had simple clothes and children had few toys. Many working-class children worked in factories or mines.

SCHOOL DAYS

Just after he turned eight, Winston went away to a boarding school. His first school, St George's, was not far from London. Winston started halfway through the term, after the other children were already settled in. The headmaster, or principal, was known for beating the boys. Winston himself was flogged for stealing sugar and tearing up the headmaster's hat. He wrote, "How I hated this school, and what a life of anxiety I lived for more than two years. I made very little progress at my lessons, and none at all at games [sports]. I counted the days and hours to the end of every term . . ."

Winston was very good at some subjects and less good at others. He could do very well when he was interested and applied himself, especially in English and history. Sometimes he was first in the class, and other times last. His school years must have been frustrating for him, his teachers, and his parents. As he grew up, he knew what he wanted to be: a politician and a soldier. He was always ready to learn useful things to help reach these goals, so he learned world history, military history, and how to give rousing speeches. He was a natural leader, known by his schoolmates for his intelligence, bravery, magnetism, and charm. He also enjoyed listening to music and singing, and loved singing patriotic songs and hymns for his entire life.

When Winston was a child, people wrote letters to stay in touch. There was no telephone or email, and sending telegrams was expensive. The postal system in Britain was excellent, making up to ten mail deliveries a day. People often wrote letters daily to report what was going on in their lives. Winston wrote letters to his parents from the age of seven. In most of them, he told of his progress at school, and asked them to come visit. He clearly felt lonely, as many children at boarding schools did (and still do). He relished visits from his parents, Jack, and Mrs. Everest. As he grew older, many of his letters explain why he was always short of cash and needed more money.

In the summer of 1882, Winston's grandfather, the 7th Duke of Marlborough, died. Lord Randolph was very upset. He took Winston and Lady Randolph to a spa town in Austria-Hungary to recover. It was Winston's first trip to Europe. Lord Randolph's brother Blandford became the 8th Duke of Marlborough.

In 1884, Winston left St George's and moved to a new school as a result of his many health problems. He was prone to falls, perhaps because he had ear trouble that led to problems balancing. He suffered his first concussion at the age of four after falling off a donkey and being kicked in the head. Although he later learned to ride and became an excellent horseman, he had some major falls. Winston also had serious bouts of pneumonia and other illnesses. As a child, he started taking his temperature every day and got alarmed if it changed much. Mrs. Everest wrote often when Winston was at school, advising him on how to keep healthy and trying to look after him even from far away.

This is a letter Winston wrote to his mother about life at school.

Winston's new school was in Brighton, a town on England's south coast. At the time, many people thought sea air helped cure illness. Winston was much happier at his new school. He thought the teachers were kind and sympathetic. He learned to swim and ride well. He did better in his classes but still came last in the class on "Conduct." However, the sea air didn't stop Winston from getting pneumonia. When he was eleven, he almost died during a bad attack in March. He wasn't well enough to return to school until July.

When Winston was at school in Brighton, his father came to town to give political speeches twice, but did not visit his son. Winston wrote to him, "I cannot think why you did not come to see me, while you were in Brighton. I was very disappointed but I suppose you were too busy to come." Despite the fact that he didn't see his father much,

Schooling for Boys

The government set up schools for all children aged five to ten. Upper-class boys in Britain were usually sent to live at private, all-male boarding schools around age six or seven. They would go on to private, all-male schools that would get them ready for attending a university or joining the military. After that they could be officers, ministers, lawyers, politicians, or managers of the family estate. Rich girls were usually taught by tutors at home and studied fewer academic subjects than boys. They learned how to run a household, paint, and do needlework. They would usually marry in their twenties. Working-class children of both sexes had little time for school because they were expected to help earn money for the family.

Winston followed his father's political career very closely, mostly through newspaper reports. He wrote letters to his father about the news and what he thought of it. Lord Randolph held several important government offices in 1885 and 1886, but then resigned from the government in 1886. He quickly fell into ill health himself, traveled a lot and tried to get back into power, but his health continued to worsen.

HARROW AND SANDHURST

In 1887, Winston began studying for the entrance exams to Harrow, one of Britain's most prestigious boarding schools. Harrow is difficult to get into, and Winston had to take tough exams. When he took the final entrance exam in March of 1888, he passed, but he got very sick on the train afterwards from the stress. He wrote to his mother, "I am longing to go to Harrow, it is such a nice place. . . . You will be able to come & see me in the summer, it is so near to London you can drive . . . in an hour & 15 minutes or so." He was accepted.

At Harrow, Winston learned both academic and military skills. He sang in the choir and conducted the band. He performed military drills and fought mock battles with the cadets. He won an important fencing championship. He won prizes for some of his schoolwork, but did poorly in other subjects. His behavior was still a problem. One teacher in charge of him wrote to his mother that he was "Constantly late for school, losing his books . . . he is so regular in his irregularity that I really don't know what to do; and sometimes think he cannot help it."

When Winston was sixteen his parents decided to fire Mrs. Everest. Jack was eleven and didn't need a nurse any longer. Winston was very upset, as was Mrs. Everest. He got her a job with his grandmother in her London house so he could still see her often.

In November of 1882, Lord Randolph's brother Blandford died. Winston's cousin, Charles Churchill, was twenty years old. Nicknamed "Sunny," he became the 9th Duke of Marlborough.

After graduating from Harrow, Winston planned a career in the military. He struggled to pass the entrance exam to Royal Military College, Sandhurst, the school for infantry and cavalry officers. After three tries, he was accepted.

While he excelled in some activities and courses at Harrow, Winston continued to have problems in school, such as being late to class.

TWO

Enter the Army

Winston Churchill started at Sandhurst in the autumn of 1893. He was delighted to be at the college and planned to do well and work hard. He wrote to his father, "The discipline here is very strict—far stricter than Harrow. . . . No excuse is ever taken—not even the pleas of 'didn't know' after the first few hours: and of course no such thing as unpunctuality or untidyness is tolerated. Still there is something very exhilarating in the military manner in which everything works: and I think I shall like my life here during the next 18 months very much."

Winston's father was suffering more from his illness, which medical historians believe was most likely a brain tumor. He was often confused and started to slur his words. He wrote Winston truly nasty letters about his behavior and even got his age and where he went to school wrong. Winston was deeply upset by his father's letters but he kept following his career and idolizing him. He didn't know how sick his father was.

Winston (left) found the military life at Sandhurst exciting. Here he is dressed in his cadet uniform with friends Lord Dillon and Bertie Cook.

When Lord Randolph was feeling better, he was kind to Winston, but then would get worse again.

Winston did very well at Sandhurst. He made friends who stayed close to him his entire life. Winston studied military strategy and tactics, how to make strong defenses, maps and mapmaking, military law, and the everyday details of running an army. He wrote to his father, "The work here is very interesting and extremely practical. . . . Shot and shell of all kinds—bridges, guns, field and siege, mapping, keeping regimental savings bank accounts, inspecting meat etc." As he went along, he took riding lessons and was first in the riding class. He had started as an infantry officer who fights on foot. Now he wanted to change to the cavalry, but his father said no. Cavalry officers fight on horseback, and have to pay for their horses and stabling, which is very expensive. Winston's parents were always short of money.

In the winter of 1893, Winston's grandmother fired Mrs. Everest, saying she didn't need her anymore. Winston was very angry but had no way to stop Mrs. Everest from losing her job with the family. They still stayed in close contact, writing letters and visiting each other regularly.

Lord Randolph became so ill that his doctor said he should retire from Parliament and take a round-the-world trip with Lady Randolph to try and get better. They returned at the end of 1894, but Lord Randolph's health worsened. He died with his family around him at home on January 24, 1895. He was almost forty-six years old.

Sadly, later that year, Mrs. Everest fell ill. Winston raced to her house and got his own doctor to come, but it was of no use. Winston was there when she died. He arranged the funeral, ordered flowers to be sent from his mother, and went himself. He wrote, "I shall never know such a friend again. . . . I never realized how much poor old Woom was to me." Winston had lost his childhood caregiver and his father in a short time.

WHAT NEXT?

Winston Churchill finished near the top of his class at Sandhurst. At the end of February, he was given his first commission as a cavalry officer. He was a second lieutenant with the 4th Hussars, in charge of thirty men. He had more free time and mostly spent it playing polo. Even after spending such a short time as an officer, Churchill was growing convinced that politics, not soldiering, was his future. "It is a fine game to play—the game of politics," he wrote to his mother. He had an incredible amount of restless energy and started chasing after fame and honor in earnest.

Churchill served as a second lieutenant with the 4th Hussars.

At the end of 1895, Churchill went to Cuba with a friend to see the war between the Spanish and the Cubans, who were fighting for their independence from Spain. He was asked by the head of Military Intelligence to find out how well the new bullets they were fighting with worked. Traveling to Cuba, he went through New York and had a great time. He was impressed by the way Americans were practical, welcoming, and without the same slavish devotion to tradition as the British. In Cuba, Churchill joined the Spanish forces and saw his first combat. He wrote five short articles for a newspaper in London, explaining the situation as he saw it. He was optimistic that a compromise could be reached that would make both sides happy. This kind of clear-seeing attitude was a hallmark of Churchill's later negotiations for the British government.

Churchill's journalistic efforts were a success. He wanted journalism to make him famous and wealthy. He kept writing from that time forward, constantly working on articles, speeches, books, or broadcasts. He started to support himself with the money he earned from his writing. He had expensive taste and lived a lavish lifestyle, but he had inherited little money from his father and had only a small salary as a soldier.

Churchill tried to get to Egypt, Greece, or South Africa to work as a journalist or soldier but failed. Instead, in September 1896, he went to India with his regiment. India bored him. He had little work to do, had about thirteen servants, and spent a great deal of time playing polo and reading history books.

BATTLES AND BOOKS

In the summer of 1897, Churchill gave his first political speech in Bath while on leave in England. He decided to stay in the army for two more years before running for election to Parliament. Soon after his speech, he

The British Empire

During the days of Queen Victoria's reign, the British Empire covered a quarter of the world. One of Britain's great strengths was its navy, which helped it to manage Australia and Britain's many colonies. Travel was slow and dangerous, mostly by ship, train, and horse. It took weeks or months to reach some parts of the empire. British politicians were educated at home then sent abroad to run these other countries. In 1900, the empire was at its largest. Today, Britain has given control of most of its colonies back to native people. Most countries that were part of the British Empire belong to an organization called the commonwealth. For a few, such as Canada, Australia, and New Zealand, the queen remains the official monarch or head of state.

went back to India because fighting had begun on the northwest frontier between India and Afghanistan. Churchill wanted to go to the front as a soldier and as a war correspondent for a London newspaper. He asked his mother to find him a paper to write for and headed straight to the frontier. Most of his fellow officers were content to let action come to them, but Churchill always pursued it.

Churchill joined the battle forces in September. He was exhilarated by battle and military strategy. He saw a great deal of combat and won a medal for his bravery under fire. But he learned that battle could also be ugly. He saw men blown apart by bullets, and he himself came close to being killed many times. Churchill thought of battle as a splendid game and stuck to his beliefs in how this game ought to be played. He thought that the soldiers deserved strong leaders, who in turn deserved loyalty. He always had respect for the soldiers fighting for the other side if they behaved well and showed loyalty to their leaders.

Churchill's first book was about the fighting he had seen on the frontier, and what he thought of the government's part in it. *The Story of the Malakand Field Force* was published in 1898, and it was well liked. Even the prime minister of the time read it and met Churchill to tell him how much he had enjoyed it.

Churchill went on to join the 21st Lancers in Egypt in August of 1898. They rode to Omdurman, near Khartoum in the Sudan. Churchill, who had obtained an assignment there as a war correspondent for a newspaper, acted as a scout. He told Sir Herbert Kitchener, the commander of the Egyptian army, how close the enemy forces were. He fought in the last great cavalry charge the British army made in Omdurman. Despite being in the thick of battle, Churchill was not even slightly wounded. He was later horrified by the way wounded soldiers were treated by their enemies and comrades alike. He saw thousands of wounded men left to die where they fell, thirsty and in great pain in the hot sun. He described the scenes in his next book, *The River War,* which he wrote during 1898 and 1899 and was published at the end of 1899.

This painting shows the charge of the 21st Lancers at Omdurman.

THREE

The Young Statesman

In 1899, Churchill made his entry into politics. He ran in an election to replace the member of Parliament (M.P.) for Oldham, who had died. Oldham is in the north of England. Churchill lost by 1,300 votes. After his defeat, Churchill turned once again to journalism. He set off for South Africa to observe the war against the Dutch settlers there, called the Boers. He was one of the first journalists on the scene that November. He roamed around near Ladysmith, a town under siege with British troops trapped inside. Because most troops and supplies moved by train, keeping the train lines open was vital. Churchill went on an armored train with an officer friend of his and 150 soldiers to try to get as close to Ladysmith as they could to see the condition of the train lines. On the way, Boer soldiers ambushed them, and part of the train was derailed.

Churchill bravely helped organize the troops to clear the track. It took an hour under heavy fire. Then he helped load the wounded into the engine and sent it to safety. He walked back to help out the remaining soldiers, but was captured along with the rest of the men by the Boers. Suddenly, Churchill was a prisoner of war. He was held in Pretoria with the others. After almost a month of imprisonment, he escaped over a wall by the toilets. Two others were supposed to escape with him, but they didn't have a chance to climb the wall.

Alone, unable to speak the local language, and without a map, Churchill decided that the only way to freedom was to try his best to get to friendly land 300 miles (484 kilometers) away. He simply walked to the nearest railway, jumped aboard a train as it pulled out of the station, and hid. By the time he jumped off again, the word was out that he had escaped, and the Boers were looking for him. Luckily, he found a British mine manager to help him when he was too hungry and thirsty to go on. He hid in the dark in a mine for three days. Then he was hidden in some bales of wool and was loaded onto another train. He emerged two days later when the train reached the first friendly station. He leapt out and went to the British consul.

Churchill wrote articles about his adventures that made him famous in Britain. He stayed in South Africa and fought the Boers. In March 1900, he wrote an article in which he said, "While

This poster was issued by the Boers for the capture of Churchill after he escaped.

we continue to [fight] . . . with tireless energy . . . we must also make it easy for the enemy to accept defeat. . . . Beware of driving men to desperation." The brutality of the British approach to the Boer War was very controversial. However, Churchill always resisted the urge to hate the enemy and make their lives too hard after war was over. He felt that a just peace gave people the chance to start their lives over with honor.

ELECTED AT TWENTY-FIVE

When Churchill returned home in July 1900, he attended his mother's wedding to her second husband, Captain George Cornwallis-West. Captain Cornwallis-West was only sixteen days older than Churchill.

The Parliamentary System

The British Parliament has two houses: the Commons and the Lords. Members of Parliament are elected to the House of Commons at general elections or when an M.P. leaves. The monarch asks the leader of the party with the most seats in the House of Commons to form a government. That leader is called the prime minister. General elections must be held at least every five years. However, if a prime minister loses support, an election can happen sooner. The prime minister appoints ministers to help run the country. The ministers are part of the prime minister's cabinet. In 1900, M.P.s weren't paid a salary, but ministers were. In 1900, only some people born into upper-class families and others who were made lords and ladies by the monarch could sit in the House of Lords. At this time, the approval of both Houses was needed to make new laws.

In 1900, Churchill published three books. The first was his only novel, *Savrola,* about an army officer fighting during a fictional war. The others were *London to Ladysmith via Pretoria* and *Ian Hamilton's March* about his time in the Boer War. By then, he had earned about £10,000 from his writing, which is worth about $750,000 today.

At the 1900 general election, Churchill won the vote in Oldham to become an M.P. for the Conservative Party. He promptly went on a three-month lecture tour all over Britain, the United States, and Canada. He met Mark Twain, President William McKinley, and Theodore Roosevelt. He returned home right after Queen Victoria died and gave his first speech in the House of Commons on February 28, 1901.

Practicing in the Bathtub

Churchill worked hard to improve his public speeches, practicing them on friends and even while taking a bath. Each speech was carefully written and rewritten, marked up and retyped until he thought it was ready. His speeches looked like poems with each line ending where he thought he would pause. Each line was indented, building up to the climax of the thought. Then the next paragraph or thought would be spaced well below the previous one.

Churchill had a speech impediment called a lisp, making him slur his "s" sounds. As his career progressed, people got to know him for this. His speeches were clear, arguments were well presented, and supporting facts were well chosen. He had a knack for explaining complicated ideas in simple terms and using emotional language to get people to feel strongly about his subject.

From the beginning, Churchill was a loud and controversial voice in politics. He was known immediately for his speeches and for his strong convictions. He argued for a reduction in spending on the military and warned of the dangers if war should break out in Europe. In May 1901 he said, "A European War cannot be anything but a cruel, heartrending struggle, which, if we are ever to enjoy the bitter fruits of victory, must demand, perhaps for several years, the whole manhood of the nation, the entire suspension of peaceful industries, and the concentrating to one end of every vital energy in the community." His outspokenness won admiration even from his opponents, like the social reformer Beatrice Webb, who wrote this about him in 1903: "[He has] no notion of scientific research, philosophy, literature or art, still less of religion. But his pluck, courage, resourcefulness and great tradition may carry him far." He could be rude and seldom did the right thing socially. He didn't mind causing inconvenience or trouble. He could also turn the

Churchill took his role as an M.P. seriously, speaking out about issues that were important to him and sharing his concerns about the state of Britain.

full light of his attention on people who caught his interest and dazzle them with it. He was absolutely sure that he was born to lead and would do a great job, given the chance. In 1906, he said to Violet Asquith, a new friend, "We are all worms. But I do believe I am a glow-worm."

Socially, Churchill began to spend time with Liberal politicians. He liked their way of thinking. He spoke out for issues he believed in, even though his own Conservative Party did not support them. For example, he started campaigning for improving social conditions for the poor in Britain. Many houses were in awful condition. Children often did not eat well and grew up malnourished. Many women died in childbirth, and many children died young, making families unstable. If the main money earner lost his job or was hurt, the family had no way to survive.

Political Parties

In 1900, Britain had three major political parties: Liberal, Conservative, and Labour. Three main issues divided the parties. First, the Liberals wanted free trade, which meant there would be no taxes placed on goods imported from abroad. The Conservatives wanted protectionism, or the taxation of goods as they came into the country so that British industry would be protected. Labour was more concerned with the rights of workers and trade unions than questions of trade. Second, political control of Ireland was a huge issue. The Conservatives wanted to keep ruling all of the country from England, while the Liberals wanted to make a compromise that would make the Irish happy. Third, the Liberals and Labour were determined to do something about the poverty and social problems that existed in England, while the Conservatives resisted changes to the class structure.

There was no system of health care or welfare to help the poor. Because education was expensive or hard to find and children were needed to earn money for the family, there was little hope of children getting educated and raising themselves out of poverty. In one of his first letters on the subject, he wrote, "I see little glory in an Empire which can rule the waves and is unable to flush its sewers." Although he wanted social changes, Churchill hated the Labour Party and socialism his whole life. He said "Socialism seeks to pull down wealth; Liberalism seeks to raise up poverty." Socialism is an economic and political theory that wants government control of industry and the distribution of wealth. However, it was because of the issue of free trade, not social change, that made Churchill leave the Conservatives and join the Liberal Party in 1904.

GOVERNMENT MINISTER

In the general election of 1905, the Conservatives were defeated, and a Liberal prime minister was appointed. Churchill was given his first government post as under-secretary of state at the Colonial Office. He started working on a constitution

In the early 1900s, many poor people lived in rundown buildings and apartments without enough food to survive. This photograph shows what one slum looked like in London at the time.

for South Africa. In January 1906, there was a general election and Churchill won as a Liberal M.P. for Manchester. He later switched to a seat in Dundee, Scotland. When he went on a vacation to Europe that summer, he visited the German emperor and saw the German army give a display.

Churchill believed that the British Empire was a great help to its poorer colonies. Like many of his contemporaries, he thought that people of color were not as intelligent or capable as white people were. He believed that the influence of the British way of life would help the colonists improve their lives. Churchill worked hard at the Colonial Office, traveled often, and learned a great deal about Britain's different lands.

This is a photographic and illustrated essay of Winston and Clementine's wedding day in 1908, which appeared in *The Sphere*.

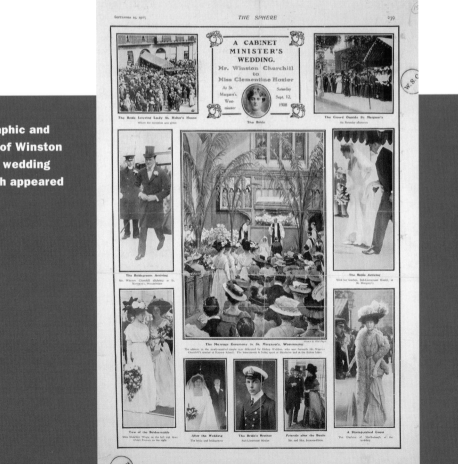

In 1908, Churchill was moved to a new job, president of the Board of Trade, by the new Liberal Prime Minister Herbert Asquith. This was a cabinet post, a much more powerful position. The Board of Trade was the government's voice in industrial matters. Churchill started to make some of the social changes he wanted by changing the laws that affected workers. He founded labor exchanges, where employers could post information about jobs, and workers could find out about them and apply for them. He also got minimum wages and conditions set in some industries. He introduced the beginnings of far-reaching reforms, such as national unemployment insurance, old-age pensions, and sickness insurance.

Churchill's political and writing careers left him little time for romance. However, in March 1908, he met Clementine Hozier for the second time in four years. Clementine was a strong, independent, beautiful woman. Like Winston, she was a liberal in politics. They wrote letters and started courting seriously. On August 11, while visiting Blenheim Palace, Churchill asked her to marry him. Their engagement was announced on August 15, and the wedding was set for September 12. Despite being quickly arranged, there were 1,300 guests at the wedding! Their first child, Diana, was born in July of 1909. Clementine had a hard time giving birth, and she had to go away to recover her strength.

THE HOME SECRETARY

In 1910, Asquith and the Liberals won another general election, with Churchill holding his Dundee seat. Asquith gave Churchill a promotion, this time to home secretary. This is one of the most important jobs in the cabinet. Churchill was responsible for police, prisons, the fire service, voting laws, immigration laws, and decisions on death penalties. He also had to write a report of every day's business in the House of Commons for the king. He loved this job, writing long, chatty letters by hand and adding lots of his personal feelings in them.

While Churchill was home secretary, there were a number of problems between workers and employers. Sometimes both sides became angry, and riots and fighting developed. The home secretary was asked to send in troops or police officers to help restore order. However, bringing armed men into a riot often made the violence worse, not better. Churchill was accused of being too eager to let soldiers get involved, though he resisted this and tried to bring the situations under control by using as little force as possible. Churchill pushed through laws making working conditions better for miners and shop workers. He also made life in the prisons better. He did not favor giving women the vote, though many pushed hard to be given this right. Churchill didn't want to yet, but thought it was a good idea in general.

There was another general election at the end of 1910, and Churchill and the Liberals won again. Soon after, he became personally involved in a fight to capture a gang of robbers who had killed two police officers and holed up in a house on Sidney Street in London. Churchill went to the scene while the siege was occuring. He sent

Voting

In 1900, only about one-sixth of the British population could vote. The vote was limited to men who had jobs or who owned land. In 1918, women were allowed to vote for the first time, after a long and often violent struggle. In 1970, almost everyone over the age of eighteen was allowed to vote.

soldiers in to help the police get the robbers out. After killing another police officer, the robbers were killed when the house caught on fire. Churchill gave the order to let the house burn down. Afterward, other politicians and the public said he behaved badly in going to the scene at all, since he was at risk. Despite his concern over the loss of life, he thought the experience was very exciting.

FIRST LORD OF THE ADMIRALTY

In July 1911, Churchill became convinced that Germany posed a threat to Britain. He started working on the nation's defense at once, putting guards on stores of explosives and making battle plans. In October, Prime Minister Asquith made Churchill First Lord of the Admiralty, in charge of the British navy. Churchill requested more money to bring the naval fleet up to a higher standard. He changed the fuel used in the ships from coal to oil, which made them travel much faster. He gave them bigger and more powerful guns. He got the sailors' pay increased. He had many more ships built to keep up with the Germans, who were building many ships. He believed that a strong navy was important to Britain's ability to win a war.

In May of 1911, Churchill's son, Randolph, was born. The family lived in a house in London at the time. The First Lord got a house with the job, but many servants were needed to run it, and the Churchills didn't have a great deal of money. Churchill spent more than he earned, even though he hadn't gotten any big book deals while he was busy working in government. Clementine was always worried about money, and Churchill thought he could write his way out of any problems. After eighteen months, they moved into Admiralty House.

Churchill was a huge fan of the newly invented airplane. He believed that airplanes would change the way wars were fought. He brought airplanes to the navy and even started learning to fly himself. In 1913, flying was very dangerous. He was involved in a number of near misses, and one of his teachers was killed while flying. Clementine made him promise to stop in 1914. He gave it up for her, although only temporarily.

Churchill enjoys some playtime with his son, Randolph, and his wife, Clementine.

FOUR

The First World War

In August 1914, Britain went to war with Germany. Winston Churchill had quietly gotten the navy ready beforehand. When war broke out, he was praised for his understanding of the situation. At first, he was seen as a great help to the government. For the navy, the war was mostly about keeping supply lines at sea open and enemy ships safely holed up in their own harbors. Churchill's navy did this well. Then German ships won a major naval battle in the Pacific Ocean and began shelling British towns on the North Sea. By autumn, Churchill was not as popular.

Some of Churchill's adventures had little to do with the navy. On October 3, 1914, Churchill was sent to Antwerp, Belgium. The Belgian government and armed forces had escaped to Antwerp as the Germans advanced through the country. If they left, the Germans would gain control of a useful port and would have totally overrun Belgium. Churchill's mission was to get the Belgians to hold out until British forces could arrive.

He tried to boost morale and fire up the tired, unhappy soldiers and officers. He enjoyed the challenge and kept them going for four days. Then the British military commander arrived, and Churchill went home. The delay bought time for the British to fortify the more important port of Dunkirk. When Antwerp fell on October 10, Dunkirk was safe. Many reporters and politicians didn't understand why Churchill was in Antwerp. He was criticized for leaving the Admiralty without a leader. He was blamed for the soldiers' deaths during the battles in Antwerp.

As Churchill reached England on October 7, his third child, Sarah, was born. He stopped in to see her and Clementine before going on to London and back to work. During the war, Churchill didn't see much of his family. They mostly stayed in the country while he worked long hours in the Admiralty House.

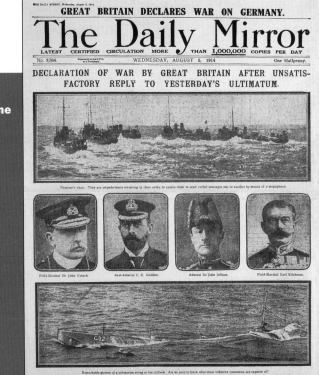

A British newspaper headline announces Britain's entrance into World War I.

One of the things Churchill was criticized for was the way he grew more and more interested in non-naval war strategies. He felt he had to do as much as he could to help his country win, and he had very big ideas. He set up the first armored car and air squadrons as part of the navy. He based them in France. In 1915, he started looking for a way to win the war in the trenches. He thought a big armored car was the answer. If it could go right over the trenches, and if no bullets or small bombs could stop it, it could pierce the trench lines and help win the war. Major Thomas Hetherington invented such a vehicle, and Churchill started military tests for it. It became known as the tank. It was too late to help win this war, but it did help in the future.

Churchill also wanted to go around the trenches. The trenches started in Belgium and stretched across France and all the way to Switzerland. Churchill suggested going north through the Baltic Sea and attacking

How World War I Began

Europe before the war was divided into two powerful sides. Germany and Austria-Hungary were on one side. On the other were Russia and France. Britain supported France and Belgium. War first began between Austria-Hungary and Serbia in July 1914. Russia joined in to support Serbia, and France joined in to support Russia. Germany backed Austria-Hungary. In August 1914, Germany invaded Belgium, so Britain was drawn into the war. Around the same time, Turkey made a treaty with Germany. Later that year, Turkey joined the fighting on the German side. The United States joined the war on Britain's side in April of 1917. The war ended in 1918.

Germany with Britain's ally, Russia. Then he put forward plans begun by others to attack from the south, in Turkey. Germany was allied with Turkey. If Britain could defeat Turkey, it would weaken Germany. Turkey is divided in two parts, one side in Europe and the other in Asia. The Dardanelles, the narrow strait that separates the two parts, was a valuable transportation route from the Mediterranean Sea to the Black Sea. After

Trench Warfare

The main battle tactic of World War I was trench warfare. Each side dug long ditches facing each other and guarded them with earthen walls and barbed wire. The soldiers lived in the trenches and fought across the short patch of "No Man's Land" between the opposing sides. Very little land was lost or won, but many men died just holding onto their positions. Life in the trenches was awful. They were often filled with mud and were freezing in winter and baking hot in summer. Lice, rats, and diseases all thrived in the trenches. There was no rest from the constant gunfire and noise. People died constantly, and there was nowhere to bury the bodies properly.

months of discussions, it was agreed that the navy would attack in the Dardanelles. After the navy made the area safe, soldiers would land on the Gallipoli Peninsula on the European side and continue the fighting.

Usually, First Lords left day-to-day command to their professional officers. However, Churchill loved being in charge. He set up a system in which he and the top officer in the navy gave most of the actual battle commands. This means he was held responsible when things went wrong. In 1914, he was in charge of 1,000 ships and 150,000 men.

When the naval battle in the Dardanelles began in February 1915, Lord Kitchener, who was in charge of the army, cut the number of soldiers pledged to attack by land. He thought the Turkish soldiers would not put up much of a fight. Churchill was very upset and thought the whole plan might fail as a result. After a few days, the naval attack was stopped. Kitchener and Churchill kept changing their minds about the best way forward. The fighting began again in March. Tragically, the Turkish waters were more heavily mined than expected, and the Turkish soldiers fought well. The British forces made little progress on land or sea. Britain and its allies sent in about 480,000 troops. More than half of them were killed. Defeated, British forces pulled out in January 1916. For the rest of his life, Churchill was blamed for the whole disaster, even though he wasn't solely responsible for it. Prime Minister Asquith also didn't help clear his name when he had the chance.

LOSING POWER

In May 1915, Liberal Prime Minister Asquith decided to form a new coalition government with the Conservatives. Both sides agreed to work together, but the Conservatives demanded that Churchill leave the Admiralty. He was made chancellor of the Duchy of Lancaster, a job without much power. He felt "forty and finished," as he put it. He was still serving on the War Council but showed his frustration and depression. Clementine said that she thought he would "die of grief." After he was taken off the War Council in November, Churchill resigned from the government. He was still an M.P., but that position was not enough on its own for him.

During this bad time, Churchill learned to paint. He was not an admirer of art, but his sister-in-law Gwendeline showed him how to paint in watercolors one day, and he was hooked. He quickly switched to oil paints and spent the rest of his life working hard to improve his skills. He always went to the top people in any field, and therefore asked for help from the best painters he could find. Painting helped Churchill relax. Although he was never considered a great painter, he was later good enough to have his work exhibited at the Royal Academy, which is considered a high honor.

Two weeks after he resigned, Churchill went to join the war on the Western Front in Belgium and France. He went as a major and trained

The battle in the Dardanelles was a disaster for Britain and France. More than 200,000 soldiers lost their lives.

in the trenches on the front line. Churchill was happy to be exposed to the hazards of war again. He was given command of a battalion, the 6th Royal Scots Fusiliers. He often spoke with the top commanders in the area, but spent his day-to-day energies in leading his own group of men. They spent six days in the trenches, then six days just behind the front line in reserve. All their efforts focused on holding a 1,000-yard (914-meter) long section of the front.

Churchill quickly won the men's loyalty, partly because he declared war on lice. In a short time, he had deloused everyone and everything, which made the soldiers' lives more comfortable.

In March 1916, Churchill went to London while on leave and spoke in Parliament. His time in London made him hungry for political power again. When he returned to the front, he wrote to Clementine to ask her to keep looking for opportunities for him to return to the government or to get a more important command in the war. Clementine felt frustrated, too, because she worried about his safety on the front, his state of mind, and his chances of returning to power. All this worry and work left them little time to spend alone to enjoy each others' company and quiet family life.

In May 1916, Churchill's battalion was combined with another because neither had enough men left alive to continue alone. Another man was put in charge, so Churchill left the military. Two days later, he was back in Parliament, making speeches. He spent the next fourteen months trying to clear his name in regard to the Dardanelles disaster and to get back into power. Finally, in July 1917, his friend and now-Prime Minister David Lloyd George appointed him to an important office. Churchill was made minister of munitions, responsible for making and supplying all the guns, ammunition, and equipment the military needed to fight the war. He had to stand for reelection in Dundee immediately and won by a large margin.

Churchill bought a house called Lullenden in Sussex, south of London, in the spring of 1917. It was expensive, but the family enjoyed life there. They kept rabbits and explored its 100 acres (40.5 hectares) of woods. Churchill usually slept in his office in London and returned to the family at Lullenden on weekends.

Churchill made changes in the way munitions were manufactured. He resolved most of the strikes and labor problems that had led to delays. His factories made, as he said, "masses of guns, mountains of shells and clouds of aeroplanes." Churchill traveled to France a great deal during the final year of the war, visiting the commanders and seeing the major battles for himself. He claimed to want to see how his munitions performed, but it is likely that he just wanted to be in on the action.

THE END OF THE WAR

The defeat of the Germans in 1918 was a surprise. Many people thought the war would go on into 1919. However, peace was declared on November 11, 1918. About 750,000 British troops had died, but about 3 million were left alive on the battlefields. Now the problem was getting all the troops home swiftly. After the general election at the end of 1918, Prime Minister George made Churchill the secretary of state for war and air.

The year 1918 was busy for Churchill personally. In June, Churchill's mother remarried again. Her marriage to George Cornwallis-West had ended in 1913. Lady Randolph's new husband, Montagu Porch, was three years younger than Churchill. September saw Winston and Clementine's tenth wedding anniversary. On November 15, their fourth child, Marigold, was born.

In his new job, Churchill changed the old system for bringing soldiers home. He made the rules fairer and brought almost one million men home by the end of January 1919. He started taking flying lessons again but stopped after he had a crash that frightened Clementine again. He also kept an army in Europe big enough to enforce the peace terms of the Treaty of Versailles. The treaty demanded that Germany pay the nations it had fought tremendous sums of money. The treaty also granted German territory to other nations and limited the size of its military. Churchill supported a just peace that didn't punish Germany too harshly for its wartime sins. He was afraid that the Treaty of Versailles was too hard on the countries that lost, not giving them the chance to rebuild and look after their own people in peacetime.

November 11 is now known as Armistice Day, marking the end of World War I. When the news of the signing of the armistice, or agreement between opponents, was announced, people took to the streets to celebrate.

Russia had been Britain's ally, but left the war in 1917 after the Bolshevik Revolution brought it under communist control. Churchill hated the Bolsheviks, who were to him the worst kind of socialists. Britain had to decide what to do with its troops in Russia. Churchill thought they should support the Russian anti-Bolshevik forces. During a year of fighting in Russia and arguing in the Commons, Britain ended up sending arms and supplies, but bringing home its troops. By the end of 1919, the British forces were out of Russia, but the Bolsheviks had won the country and created the Soviet Union. Churchill was bitterly disappointed and feared the destruction that communist Russia would bring. He was once again made fun of in the media and by the public for his obsession with fighting the Bolsheviks.

During 1920, Churchill kept his crusade against the Bolsheviks going. He also tried to help with the ongoing crisis in Ireland. Ireland was torn apart. One side wanted to put an end to British rule, and the other side wanted London to keep control of the country. Churchill sided with those wanting British rule and got drawn deeper into the conflict.

The League of Nations

The League of Nations was created by the peace agreement that ended World War I. Its purpose was to help countries work together for peace. The countries agreed that they would discuss their problems before they went to war. It started well, with many countries signing up. However, by the 1930s, it was unable to stop Germany, Japan, and Italy from attacking other countries. The League of Nations was officially disbanded in 1945, but it had already lost all authority when World War II began in 1939.

FIVE

Roaring Through the Twenties

In 1920, much of the Middle East was under British rule. The region was expensive to run. At the beginning of 1921, Winston Churchill was given a new government position as secretary of state for the colonies. He was in charge of all the British colonies, but had the special task of cutting the cost of running the colonies of Iraq, Palestine, and Arabia in half. He planned to remove a great number of the British-born ministers ruling in these countries and replace them with mostly native-run governments. Churchill was sympathetic to the idea of creating a Jewish national homeland in Palestine, though he did not at that time want to create a separate Jewish nation like today's Israel.

The other great issue for Churchill to deal with was the unrest in Ireland. Each side was fighting and murdering members of the other.

The Irish were divided over religion. In the south, an area called Eire was mainly Catholic. The north, made up of six of Ireland's thirty-two counties and known as Ulster, was mostly Protestant. After long discussion, an agreement was reached to divide Ireland into two parts. The southern part would be entirely separate from Britain. It would rule itself. The northern part, now called Northern Ireland, would have a local government, but would be ruled overall by Britain. Churchill was credited with having worked out the compromise treaty, which kept peace for fifty years.

In March 1921, Churchill traveled to Egypt to attend the Cairo conference. On the first five camels, from the left: Clementine and Winston Churchill, the famous near east writer and authority Gertude Bell, Lawrence of Arabia, and Churchill's longtime bodyguard Walter H. Thompson.

UPS AND DOWNS

Although his political career was going well, 1921 was a hard year for Churchill personally. His mother fell down a flight of stairs at the end of May and experienced medical complications as a result. A month later, she died at age sixty-seven. Churchill wrote, "I do not feel a sense of tragedy, but only of loss. Her life was a full one."

While Churchill was very busy politically, he spent a lot of time away from Clementine and their children. A great deal of their marriage was spent apart, but they wrote many letters and stayed close to each other in thought. Clementine also traveled, visiting friends and resting to restore her health. Tutors and nurses cared for their children. Both parents were away in August when Marigold got sick. Winston and Clementine went to be with her. She was two and a half years old, and had been a bright and active little girl. She died after ten days, with both her parents by her side. Winston and Clementine were grief-stricken. Winston went to Scotland to recover. Clementine stayed in London with the other children, where they were soon struck by influenza. Fortunately, all recovered safely.

Even though he was busy with his job, Churchill found time to write his war memoir, *The World Crisis*. Started during 1921, it was published in six volumes between 1923 and 1931. Many consider this work to be Churchill's finest multivolume work.

After inheriting some money, Churchill decided to buy a new family home in the country called Chartwell House. Only 24 miles (39 kilometers) south of London, it was a more practical base and was the family's home for the rest of Churchill's life. When Winston was arranging to buy Chartwell, Clementine gave birth to their last child, Mary.

OUT OF POWER

In October 1922, it looked like Britain might go to war again with Turkey. During the crisis, Prime Minister George's coalition government collapsed. Churchill collapsed, too, with appendicitis. He had an operation on October 18 and took three weeks to recover enough to go out in public. While he was ill, the new Conservative Prime Minister Bonar Law called a general election. Clementine campaigned for her husband, but he didn't appear until right before the election on November 12. Dundee did not reelect Churchill. He came in fourth in the polls. The

The Churchill family would enjoy many years at Chartwell.

Liberals were suddenly third in Parliament, after the Conservatives and Labour.

As a friend put it, "Winston was so down in the dumps he could scarcely speak. . . . He thought his world had come to an end—at least his political world. I thought his career was over." Before starting to fight his way back into power, Churchill took his family on a long vacation in the south of France. He rested and wrote more of *The World Crisis*. He was forty-eight years old.

Churchill said, "In the twinkling of an eye I found myself without an office, without a seat [in Parliament], without a party and without an appendix." He was moving away from Liberal policies and back toward the Conservative side. During the next general election in December 1923, Churchill tried to win a Liberal seat but failed. He ran as an Independent in March 1924 and lost again.

Finally, Churchill decided to run with Conservative backing in the October general election. He won in Epping, near London. Conservative Prime Minister Stanley Baldwin asked him to be chancellor of the exchequer, in charge of the country's economic policy and budget. Churchill accepted and announced that he was going back to his first party, the Conservatives.

CONSERVATIVE CHANCELLOR

The chancellor of the exchequer holds an important post and gets an important house to go along with it. The prime minister lives at 10 Downing Street, and the chancellor at 11 Downing Street. Churchill set up his London home there. He threw himself into his new job, working on reducing income tax and making more social reforms. He wanted people to create wealth by working hard and making profits. He helped

sort out how the countries involved in World War I would pay off their war debts.

In 1925, Churchill decided to change the way Britain's money was valued. He brought the pound back to the gold standard, which meant it was backed by gold held by the government. Although the top economists working with Churchill had advised this change, it caused economic problems. It made the pound worth more, which made it harder for British industries to sell goods overseas because they cost more to foreign buyers. This led to unemployment in British industries, especially in coal mining.

In 1926, unemployment led to bad feelings between workers and employers. On May 4, the country came to a stop in the General Strike. The strike stopped newspapers from being printed except for one published by the government and one by the workers' unions. For eight days, Churchill's job was to publish the *British Gazette,* the government's newspaper. By the last day, more than 2,200,000 copies had been read. Its tone was very antiworker and antistrike. At the end of the General Strike, he tried to help the coal miners and their employers come to an agreement to end the continuing miners' strike. It took almost until the end of the year for this to happen. Churchill did many things to improve living conditions for average people. However, working people doubted him because of his actions to stop the strike and because of his hatred of socialism.

Churchill served as chancellor for four and a half years. After the strikes ended, he worked to make Britain's economy stronger. His speeches in the Commons were a great success, showing his incredible ability for writing and speaking. When a general election was called in May 1929, Churchill won again in Epping, but the Conservatives lost control of the government. For the first time, Labour had the most seats in Parliament, so a Labour prime minister took charge. Churchill was once again without a government job, but this time he was still an M.P.

The General Strike

Mine owners wanted coal miners to work longer hours for less pay. The miners would not, so the owners locked them out of the mines. Most of the other industrial workers in Britain wanted to show their support for the miners. At midnight on May 3, 1926, about three million workers, or 20 percent of all adult men, joined the General Strike. Britain fell into chaos. On May 13, everyone but the miners went back to work. In October, they too went back, accepting the original terms because they and their families faced starvation.

SIX

The Wilderness Years

By the 1930s, Winston Churchill seemed old-fashioned. He was known by everyone, had been in politics for more than three decades, and had a long history of successes and failures. He was out of fashion with the political powers because some of his views were not widely shared. He was well known for being smart and capable, but also known for being rash and impulsive. This made him a difficult person to work with because he was unpredictable. Energetic and enthusiastic, he also could be as exhausting as a small child insisting that his game be played over and over again.

For ten years, Churchill was an M.P. without a government position. He spoke openly about some unpopular policies, such as who should rule India. The Conservative Party thought it was time to give control of India's government back to its people, but Churchill thought it was too soon to do so. He was afraid that the country would fall into civil war over religious issues.

Churchill was aware of how much stronger Germany was becoming. He was afraid that Britain was falling behind Germany in military power. He got information from officers and government workers and tried to convince anyone who would listen that Britain and the rest of Europe still faced danger from Germany. However, he didn't have a good idea of how to pay for this military buildup. Britain had to spend a lot of money defending its colonies, so it didn't have much money left for building up a large military. As the years passed, Churchill also spoke out against appeasement, the policy of allowing Germany some of its demands for new land in order to avoid another war.

Churchill was also alarmed by Britain's lack of strong strategic alliances with other countries. He thought Britain should work with the United States and the Soviet Union to stop Germany's expansion. At the time, this was seen as unrealistic, but later this alliance did win the Second World War. His suggested alliance with the Soviet Union showed how

The Rise of Germany

After World War I, Germany was left poor, with little hope of building itself up again. By 1932, people were hungry, many were unemployed, and inflation was so high that money was worthless. It took a wheelbarrow of money to buy a loaf of bread! Adolf Hitler was elected chancellor in 1933 by promising to make Germany strong again. He took a cruel approach, telling people that only one way of life and racial background was acceptable, and all others had to be stamped out. His policies appealed to vast numbers of Germans. By 1935, Germany was militarily strong and desperate for power and land.

practical Churchill could be. He hated communism more than almost anything else, but grasped the bigger picture. The most important goal was keeping Germany from expanding its power. Therefore, he was willing to work with the communist Soviet Union, a lesser evil at that time, in order to reach that goal.

FRIENDS AND FAMILY

Churchill's good friends were loyal to him during his "wilderness years." He spent time at Chartwell with his family, and they entertained guests often. Some of his friends were also family favorites, such as Professor Frederick Lindemann, an Oxford physicist. He was racist and snobbish, but very good at explaining complicated science in simple terms. He played tennis with Clementine and enjoyed spending time with the children. Clementine didn't like some of Winston's other friends. Brendan Bracken, the Irish M.P. and newspaperman, was an energetic gossip who created excitement and chaos. Together with Desmond Morton and Ralph Wigram, Bracken helped Churchill stay in touch with what was going on in government.

Clementine disliked Lord Beaverbrook, the Canadian newspaper baron. He was full of energy and was driven to succeed. Lord Birkenhead was another of Churchill's friends. He was a lawyer and a quick thinker, known for remarks that were often rude and unkind. Together with Churchill, Lords Birkenhead and Beaverbrook could act as bullies and could misbehave like young boys. Churchill could be awful to his servants and friends alike. If he didn't like a situation, he could erupt with verbal abuse. He would shout over something as insignificant as the temperature of bathwater. To his credit, he liked it when people stood up to him.

Churchill went to his London apartment when Parliament was in session but lived at Chartwell the rest of the time. He also went on vacations with and without Clementine and the children. As was his habit, he usually stayed at friends' houses or took cruises on their yachts. He still worked hard while on vacation, keeping odd hours and expecting everyone else to fit his schedule.

At Chartwell, Churchill practiced bricklaying. He built a walled garden and a playhouse for Mary. Churchill also made a big lake, a swimming pool, and a waterfall, and he renovated cottages on the property. He built a studio and spent a great deal of time painting in it. Churchill loved playing with the children and was famous for his loud, rough, and inventive games. Even though he didn't have much time to spare, he wanted to be an involved parent, unlike his own had been.

Churchill wrote many articles for newspapers and magazines, worked on drafts of speeches, wrote his autobiography, *My Early Life*, and

Churchill takes a break from building Mary's playhouse. Mary stands in front of him while daughter Sarah lifts a brick.

wrote *Marlborough: His Life and Times* about his great ancestor. Churchill's other books written during the 1930s include *Thoughts and Adventures* and *Great Contemporaries.* In a letter to Baldwin, Churchill said he finished "200 bricks and 2000 words a day." Churchill had several researchers and assistants to help him.

Churchill kept odd hours, so he and Clementine had separate bedrooms. He usually woke up at 8 o'clock, but stayed in bed eating a big breakfast, sometimes more like a dinner, with wine. He dictated to a secretary for hours. He would deal with his letters and read the news before rising and having a bath. After he was dressed, he would play with the children, do some work around the house, or have talks with people. A long lunch came next, with political discussions and a great deal of food and drink. After lunch, he went back to bed for a nap, then woke to do more work. Later, he had another bath and dressed for dinner. Dinner was usually long and filled with talk, most of it from Churchill himself. He loved to bring up topics that interested him and happily took control of any discussion. After dinner he worked more, often writing his books at this late hour. He finally went to sleep around 3 o'clock.

MORE UPS AND DOWNS

In 1929, Churchill was in New York City when the stock market crashed. He saw a financially ruined man jump off a building. Churchill had most of his money tied up in the U.S. stock market, so he also faced financial hardship after the crash. He moved the family into a small cottage at Chartwell for a while. Clementine worried seriously about the cost of Chartwell and feared they might have to sell it. In 1938, after more financial difficulties, Churchill actually put Chartwell up for sale. Luckily, Sir Henry Strakosch, a financier and a supporter of Churchill's rearmament policies, rescued Chartwell by assuming responsibility for Churchill's investments.

In 1930, Churchill was made chancellor of Bristol University, which was a great honor. He loved wearing the elaborate robes for the ceremony. He enjoyed the ribbons, medals, and pendants his different offices earned him. Dressing up gave him a sense of being a special part of a great occasion.

Churchill faced some personal trials in the 1930s. In 1931, he was hit by a car while crossing a road in New York City. He was badly hurt. In 1932, he became seriously ill from eating bad food while traveling in Germany and Austria. It took him months to recover from the fever and digestive upset. In 1934, Churchill's beloved cousin "Sunny," the 9th Duke of Marlborough, died.

In 1935, King George V died, and his son became King Edward VIII. King Edward VIII was in love with an American woman who had been divorced. He decided that this woman, Wallis Simpson, must be his

Leading to a War

In 1936, Germany started to take land back that it had lost in the Treaty of Versailles. Troops went into the Rhineland. Then Hitler pushed for more land to build a new German empire. In 1938, Germany took over Austria. Next, Hitler invaded the Czech Sudetenland in September 1938. The rest of Czechoslovakia fell in March 1939. In August 1939, Germany and the Soviet Union made a pact to be allies. Hitler invaded Poland on September 1, 1939. Two days later, Britain and France declared war on Germany and its allies.

wife. Churchill put the full weight of his support behind the king. The country was not ready to have a divorced queen, so Edward was told he would have to give her up or give the crown up. He chose to give up the crown and to go into exile, married to Wallis Simpson. Churchill faced humiliation in the newspapers and Parliament because he had taken the king's side in the argument. Edward's brother was crowned King George VI in 1936.

By 1938, Britain was facing up to the reality of war with Germany. Prime Minister Neville Chamberlain had meetings with Hitler and agreed to appeasement. Although Chamberlain said he had negotiated "Peace in our time" in September 1938, Churchill didn't believe the agreement would stop Hitler from claiming more land. It was feared that London would be bombed as soon as a war began. In June 1938, the government started building bombproof rooms under a government office building between the prime minister's house and Parliament. These rooms became the Cabinet War Rooms, where the heads of the military and government could meet and make decisions in safety.

As Hitler kept claiming more territory and invaded Prague, people started to listen to Churchill again. They finally realized why he had fought to get the country prepared for war. Soon newspapers and the public were asking for him to return to government.

This cartoon shows Churchill being pestered by a German airplane. For many years, Churchill had been concerned about Germany's efforts to build up its air force. People said he had "a bee in his bonnet," meaning he wouldn't stop talking about it.

The invasion of Poland by Germany led Britain to declare war against Germany. This conflict led to what we now call World War II.

SEVEN

Back in Power

Hitler invaded Poland in the early morning of September 1, 1939. Prime Minister Chamberlain had promised to protect Poland and asked Germany to withdraw. He also asked Churchill to join the War Cabinet but didn't offer him a government office. On September 3, after hearing nothing from Hitler, Chamberlain made a radio speech saying that Britain was again at war with Germany. Britain and the nations fighting with it were known as the Allied Powers. Germany and the nations fighting with it were known as the Axis Powers.

Later that day, Chamberlain asked Churchill to take his former position of First Lord of the Admiralty. Churchill assumed this role with his usual thoroughness, taking stock of the military situation and dictating a vast quantity of memos. He was not happy because Britain was weaker than Germany on all fronts. It would take more than six months to get Britain truly ready to fight properly. However, he made some brilliant and inspiring speeches in Parliament and on the radio and helped get the British people in the proper state of mind for the long and difficult war ahead. Churchill always told people directly how bad the situation was, but then went on to tell them how he thought it would work out for the best in the end. Here's an example of a speech he gave in Parliament on November 7, 1939.

> There will not be in this war any period when the seas will be completely safe; but neither will there be, I believe and trust, any period when the full necessary traffic of the Allies cannot be carried on. We shall suffer and we shall suffer continually, but by perseverance, and by taking measures on the largest scale, I feel no doubt that in the end we shall break their hearts.

Once again, Churchill took direct control of the navy. He was blamed by some for confusing the men at sea by changing plans too often. He was also criticized for trying to use the navy to attack instead of using it to defend the merchant ships carrying supplies to Britain. Merchant ships were being attacked and often sunk by German submarines. Churchill was never able to stay out of other people's business, so he tried his best to get other departments to do what he thought was right. People criticized him for this as well.

On November 30, Churchill turned sixty-five. He had been in politics for forty years and had still not reached the highest office. He was full of energy and enthusiasm for the fight. He loved traveling to France to inspect the British troops stationed there, have meetings, and see the situation close up.

Not much happened in the first six months of the war, so it was called the "Phony War" by many British people. By April 1940, this was almost over. Hitler invaded Norway to protect his source of important iron ore in next-door Sweden. Britain was slow to respond to this invasion and didn't mount a successful counterattack. After completely failing to save Norway and beat the German forces back, British troops returned home. The next blow to the British war effort would prove to be even more severe.

PRIME MINISTER

Early in the morning of May 10, Hitler's troops invaded France, Belgium, Luxembourg, and Holland. By that evening, Prime Minister Chamberlain had resigned. The king and Chamberlain wanted Lord Halifax, the foreign secretary, to be the next prime minister, but he said no. Instead, King George VI offered the job to Winston Churchill. Churchill was in some disgrace over the Norwegian disaster, but everyone remembered how clearly he had warned the British about the German threat during the 1930s and knew he could be trusted. Churchill was delighted. He said that he was immediately "conscious of a profound sense of relief. I felt as if I were walking with destiny, and that all my past life had been but a preparation for this hour and this trial."

It is many people's opinion that this was indeed true. Most of the qualities that had made Churchill a difficult and often irritating minister made him a great prime minister. He had a knack for seeing the big picture while also focusing on the small details. He assumed that the British people would act as heroes while fighting and also while battling with the difficulties of life at home during wartime. He never let anyone think of defeat or halfheartedness. He pushed forward his schemes with enthusiasm and showed a strength of purpose. Winston Churchill let himself become a symbol of the British determination to win the war.

His unique way of doing things made him into a kind of mascot the British could depend on when times were bad.

Churchill's first speech as prime minister was short. When he came into the House of Commons, there were no great cheers. The words he spoke, however, were memorable.

> I have nothing to offer but blood, toil, tears and sweat. We have before us an ordeal of the most grievous kind. . . . You ask, what is our policy? I can say: It is to wage war, by sea, land and air, with all our might and with all the strength that God can give us; to wage war against a monstrous tyranny, never surpassed in the dark, lamentable catalogue of human crime. That is our policy. You ask, what is our aim? I can answer in one word: It is victory, victory at all costs, victory in spite of all terror, victory, however long and hard the road may be; for without victory, there is no survival.

This poster shows Churchill as a bulldog. It was meant to encourage people to be strong and hang on the way Churchill was. Together Britain could hold safe during the war.

HOLDING THE LINE!

Churchill now faced a great challenge. France was weakening under German attacks. He visited France three times and held many special War Cabinet meetings. The War Cabinet was trying to determine what Britain could do to help France resist and also what it would do if France fell. By May 25, it was clear that the Allied troops would not win in France, so they headed to the beaches at Dunkirk and Calais. It was also clear that Italy was thinking of joining Germany in the war.

Churchill's War Cabinet met and argued over whether peace should be negotiated with Germany, or if Britain should stand alone and fight to the end. Things looked bad in France, Italy seemed strong, and Germany seemed unstoppable. The War Cabinet agreed with Churchill to wait and see what happened with the troops in France. He told a meeting of all the government ministers that Britain was planning to stand firm. He is reported to have said, "If this island story of

Easy Targets

Winston Churchill moved into 10 Downing Street about a month after he became prime minister. The old building was not very strong. When London started being bombed, a new home, the No. 10 Annexe, was built above the Cabinet War Rooms. Although it was part of an office building, it was fairly comfortable and strong. Because the House of Commons is easy to spot from the air, parliamentary debates were moved to the nearby Church House. The prime minister's weekend house, Chequers, was thought to be too easy to spot during full moons. On those weekends, Churchill went to stay with friends at another country house called Ditchley Park.

Churchill's War Cabinet consisted of eight members of the British government. In the back row (left to right) are Arthur Greenwood, minister without portfolio; Ernest Bevin, minister of labor and national service; Lord Beaverbrook, minister of aircraft production; and Sir Kingsley Wood, chancellor of the exchequer. In the front row (left to right) are Sir John Anderson, lord president of the council; Winston Churchill, prime minister, first lord of the treasury, and minister of defense; Clement Attlee, lord privy seal; and Anthony Eden, secretary of state for foreign affairs.

ours is to end at last, let it end only when each one of us lies choking in his own blood upon the ground." His ministers cheered and pounded him on the back.

Within days, British troops were trapped in France and seemed sure to be captured. Churchill, along with most of the British and French military and government, thought most of the soldiers would be killed or captured. What happened next was amazing. Small sailboats, motor launches, and yachts set out from the English coast and crossed the English Channel to pick up the soldiers stranded on the beaches near Dunkirk. The boats were captained by civilian and military pilots. No one knows why, but the Germans decided not to attack them. This, along with the good weather, allowed 335,000 British and French troops to be rescued and brought safely to Britain. The whole country was delighted.

Churchill wanted his government to show determined optimism. He sent around a memo at the end of May asking that the officials keep morale high, not lie about how bad things might get, and show "confidence in our ability" to win.

THE FALL OF FRANCE

On June 4, Churchill gave a famous speech in Parliament, saying,

> We shall fight in France, we shall fight on the seas and oceans, we shall fight with growing confidence and growing strength in the air, we shall defend our island, whatever the cost may be. We shall fight on the beaches, we shall fight on the landing grounds, we shall fight in the fields and in the streets, we shall fight in the hills; we shall never surrender.

In spite of his promise to fight in France and his three more visits there, the French government surrendered to Germany on June 17. On June 18, Churchill spoke again in Parliament, saying,

> The battle of France is over, I expect that the battle of Britain is about to begin. . . . Hitler knows that he will have to break us in this island or lose the war. If we can stand up to him all Europe may be free . . . but if we fail, then the whole world, including the United States, and all that we have known and cared for, will sink into the abyss of a new dark age . . .

Churchill asked Franklin D. Roosevelt, the president of the United States, for help many times. He told him how bad things might get if Britain lost to Germany and how the United States might find itself facing a bigger and better armed foe than itself if Germany took control of all of Europe. However, the United States wasn't ready to enter the war.

Sometimes Churchill's temper flared when he was under stress. He got more impatient and rude than before. Clementine wrote only one letter to him in 1940, in June, and it said that he was in danger of "being generally disliked by your colleagues & subordinates because of your rough sarcastic & overbearing manner." In July, Churchill started to lighten up a bit, and his manner grew more relaxed.

After France surrendered, its naval ships were left in ports around the world. Churchill was determined to keep these ships out of German hands. British ships surrounded as many French ships as they could. Churchill ordered all others to be sunk. On July 3, British ships attacked French ships in the Mediterranean. About 1,300 French soldiers were killed, but Churchill showed how ruthless and strong he and Britain could be through this act. The claims that Britain would keep fighting no matter what now seemed real. M.P.s were heartened, and the French navy did not fall into German hands. The United States was impressed. It decided to send some destroyers to help Britain in September.

THE BATTLE OF BRITAIN

The German air force tried to destroy the British air force between August and October 1940 in the Battle of Britain. Both air forces had just over one thousand planes and slightly more pilots. On August 20, Churchill said, "Never in the field of human conflict was so much owed by so many to so few." Germany had the advantage of attacking, while Britain was fighting to save itself from invasion. The worst fighting took place on September 15. Churchill watched the battle until its end. Every British plane was in the air. This left the air force without reserves to replace lost people and equipment. It was a desperate and terrifying night for Britain.

Air Raids

Starting in July 1940, German airplanes bombed Britain regularly. Most air raids took place at night and targeted cities, ports, and factories making military goods. Every night, people fled into air-raid shelters in their backyards, subway stations, or in other public shelters. Thousands were killed, and homes, schools, offices, and factories were ruined. Even the House of Commons and Buckingham Palace were bombed. Those who escaped direct hits suffered from stress, fear, and chronic lack of sleep. During the eight months known as the Blitz, more than sixty thousand civilians were killed.

Every day through the summer, Britons expected invasion. Churchill toured bombed sites across the country, chomping on a cigar and twirling his hat on his walking stick. He cried at particularly awful sights, winning the hearts of the people who came to see him. People were good at helping each other out in these hard times, offering shelter, food, and support as they could. Churchill was seen as one of them, trying his hardest to keep them safe and free. Although there was no moment of triumph, the Battle of Britain was won by the British air force because it wasn't destroyed. The Germans knew they couldn't invade Britain while British planes still defended its coastline. By late autumn, it seemed that the country would not be invaded, but bombs still fell almost every night.

During the Battle of Britain, the German bomb raids did a lot of damage to British cities and ports. This photograph shows London after an attack. Notice the ruined buildings in the foreground.

EIGHT

The Tide Turns

At the beginning of 1941, President Roosevelt sent his friend and advisor Harry Hopkins to visit Britain and report back. Churchill spared no effort to show him both how brave Britain was and how much it needed U.S. help. By the end of his month-long visit, Hopkins was a big fan of Churchill.

Churchill spent a lot of time that spring visiting British cities and ports, touring the damage and giving speeches. The war was going badly. Germany took possession of Yugoslavia and Greece in April. The battles in North Africa were mostly being lost. Churchill went to Chartwell four times that June and July, even though the house was closed up. He checked on his goldfish and walked the grounds, thinking about what to do next.

On June 22, Germany attacked its ally, the Soviet Union. Suddenly, the tide of war changed. Churchill gave a radio speech that evening, saying,

Germany succeeded in attacking important government buildings through its air raids over London. Churchill tours the ruins of the House of Commons in May 1941.

No one has been a more consistent opponent of Communism for the past twenty-five years. I will unsay no word that I have spoken about it. But all this fades away. . . . We have but one aim and one single irrevocable purpose. We are resolved to destroy Hitler and every vestige of the Nazi régime. . . . Any man or state who fights against Nazidom will have our aid. . . . It follows therefore that we shall give whatever help we can to Russia and the Russian people.

The Soviet Union became a strong ally as Britain sent help, even though it cost the British a lot to do so. No one thought the Soviets could hold out for long against Germany. The United States thought about how to help, too. Hopkins went to Moscow to talk with Joseph Stalin, the Soviet leader. Stalin started pushing for Britain to attack the

Code Breaking

In a secret military camp in Bletchley Park, near Oxford, people worked feverishly to break enemy code and translate their messages. Success meant the Allies could know where the next attack was headed or where German submarines were located in the Atlantic Ocean. Germans used a machine called Enigma to encode their messages, and the settings on the machine were changed every day. The British made their first breakthrough with the German messages in May 1940. Thousands of lives, many ships, and tons of goods were saved in what is known as the Battle of the Atlantic. When the Enigma machine was changed in 1942, the British temporarily lost their ability to decode German messages, and disaster struck the Atlantic shipping routes again.

Germans in France, on a Second Front. This would help relieve the pressure on the Eastern Front, where the German and Soviet armies were fighting. The Soviet loss of life was awful. In the battle for Stalingrad alone, nearly 500,000 Soviets lost their lives. Britain helped as much as it could by sending information about German plans of attack from messages they had intercepted and decoded.

In August, Churchill met President Roosevelt at a secret meeting held on a ship in Placentia Bay, Newfoundland. They met mostly so they could get to know each other. The United States was determined to avoid joining the war as long as it could. Churchill wanted the United States to join the British war effort as soon as possible. Roosevelt and Churchill agreed on the Atlantic Charter. This was an eight-point statement about what the British and Americans wanted from the war. Even though the United States wasn't actually in the war yet, the charter went beyond agreeing that

Roosevelt and Churchill discuss the Atlantic Charter aboard the HMS *Prince of Wales*, a British battleship.

Hitler must be stopped. It included points that would apply after the war was won. These were about trade, international peacekeeping organizations, and peoples' freedom to choose their governments.

In autumn, the British forces won some victories in northern Africa and the Middle East. By this point, U.S. ships were helping a great deal in protecting the merchant ships that crossed the Atlantic, guarding them as far as Iceland. Between this help and the German messages that were decoded, the frightening Battle of the Atlantic was won for the time being. Churchill was becoming worried that Japan might enter the war. This concerned him because he had no reserves to send to the Far East to protect British land there. Japan was already fighting with the Chinese to gain Chinese land. Allied powers fighting with the Chinese were worried that Japan would use the opportunity presented by the war in Europe to take control of European colonies in the Far East.

Supplies

Keeping the British fed took a lot of work. Farmers were pushed to meet stiff quotas for food production. Most men joined the military. The government started the Women's Land Army and trained 100,000 "Land Girls" to help farm. Getting enough raw materials to make airplanes, tanks, guns, and bullets was difficult as well. People donated their pots and pans, iron fences, and anything else that could be melted down and reused. The United States sent vast amounts of food and raw materials as well as military items to help. Every merchant ship that was sunk was a disaster, both for the lives lost and for the supplies lost.

Churchill scrutinized the work his government was doing. He sent thousands of memos about his observations, asking why goals weren't met, putting forward his own ideas, and attempting to focus people on his aims. He wanted food rations to be as generous as possible and war-damage compensation payments to be made. He criticized decisions he felt were wrong or just not thorough enough. He even played with the names for new official schemes, changing the "Local Defence Volunteers" to the "Home Guard" and "Communal Feeding Centres" to "British Restaurants."

"SO WE HAD WON AFTER ALL!"

On December 7, 1941, the Japanese bombed American ships at the U.S. naval base at Pearl Harbor in Hawaii. It was a terrible surprise attack. In two hours, 21 ships were sunk or damaged, 188 aircraft were lost, and 2,403 Americans were killed. Suddenly, the United States joined in the war. Churchill was now sure that the Allies would win. He exclaimed,

The USS *Shaw* explodes after being hit by a bomb during the surprise attack by Japan on Pearl Harbor in Hawaii.

"So we had won after all!" However, the Japanese sunk two British battle-ships in the Pacific Ocean on December 9 and took control of all the oceans except the Atlantic. Churchill crossed the Atlantic, leaving on December 12 for a meeting in Washington, D.C. It was an awful journey through stormy seas. Roosevelt met Churchill in person and invited him to stay in the White House instead of at a hotel.

They discussed their joint war strategy, how to move troops, and what to do where and when. The Americans agreed that the war in Europe had to be won first, before Japan could be beaten. They immediately started using car factories and shipyards to produce vast quantities of military goods. On December 26, Churchill gave a well-received speech to Congress. That night, he had a mild heart attack while opening a window. His doctor said that he needed to rest but didn't tell him that he had suffered a heart attack. The doctor told no one. He was afraid that because Churchill couldn't take the recommended six weeks to rest, it would only cause panic if anyone knew he was not well.

Churchill gave a speech in Ottawa, Canada, and then had more meetings in Washington, D.C. He spent five days in Florida resting before returning to Washington, D.C. Because the situation in the Far East looked bad, Churchill took a twenty-two-hour flight back to Britain. The British thought his plane was an enemy plane at first, and it was almost shot down. Churchill landed safely after being away for more than a month.

Things immediately got much worse for Britain because of the Japanese. With the British colony of Singapore under threat, Churchill asked for a vote of confidence in Parliament. This means that all M.P.s vote to say if they believe the prime minister is fit to carry on in his or her job. He won the vote on January 27, 464 to 1. Then the Germans changed their code and Bletchley Park lost the ability to crack them for almost a year. At the same time, the Germans broke the Allied code saying where the shipping convoys were in the Atlantic Ocean. Heavy losses began again. On February 15, Singapore surrendered to the Japanese. Churchill was growing more concerned about how well the British troops were fighting. He thought they were "not as good fighters as their fathers were."

By the end of February, Churchill was saddened. He talked about giving up command. Clementine wrote, "He is so brave. . . . I hope his stout heart will not be broken." His daughter Mary wrote, "He is not too well physically, and he is worn down by the continuous crushing pressure of events." During April, he started to cheer up again, despite more losses in the Far East. He was working on plans for the Allied invasion of Europe with Stalin and Roosevelt. While the Allies built up the strength they needed, British engineers started working on the great floating harbors needed to land all the troops and equipment they needed on the French coast.

FIGHTING EVERYWHERE

Fighting was going on all over the world: in Europe, the Far East, North Africa, the Middle East, and the Soviet Union. Radio signals and telephone calls could be coded to a certain extent, but no communication was very safe. To agree on policy in secret, people had to meet face-to-face. To coordinate their efforts, Churchill flew to the United States again in June to meet with Roosevelt. He was gone for about ten days and faced another vote of confidence in his ability to govern in the House of Commons when he got back. Once again he won, 475 to 25.

Attacks on ships taking supplies to the Soviet Union became so frequent that Churchill stopped the shipping. Stalin was angry about this. The United States and Britain agreed that the focus of their efforts had to be

North Africa and then the Second Front in Europe. This also upset Stalin. Churchill decided he had to meet Stalin in person to explain his decisions. Churchill flew to Cairo at the beginning of August and met the commanders and troops in North Africa. He put General Montgomery in charge of the region. Then he flew on to Moscow. Both flights were very uncomfortable, and the passengers had to wear oxygen masks.

The Home Front

During the war, Britain was known as the Home Front. Civilians were as much involved in this war as soldiers were. The increasing shortages of food and clothing created the need for rationing, a complicated system of coupons or points that let every person have an equal share of what supplies were available. While no one starved, everyone was pretty hungry. All windows had to be covered with blackout curtains after dark. Hefty fines were given if even a small chink of light got through because it might attract bombers. It was difficult to travel because most gasoline and train carriages were being used by the military. Also, all the signposts and rail-station signs were taken down to confuse the Germans in case of an invasion, so it was hard to know where you were!

CLOTHING BOOK
1943-44 General CB1 6
This book must not be used until the holder's name and full postal address have been written below.
HOLDER'S NAME Lucas AV (in BLOCK letters)
ADDRESS 95- Wilton Road (in BLOCK letters)
Shirley, Bolton.

Detach this book at once and keep it safely—it is your only means of buying clothing.
HOLD PAGES I-VII IN ONE HAND AND CUT ALONG THIS LINE

Holder's National Registration No.
ECUB. 60 1
ISSUED BY
SOUTHAMPTON

THIS BOOK IS NUMBER AC 570745

FOOD OFFICE
If found, please hand in this book at any Food Office or Police Station
PAGE I

While Churchill and Stalin had very different ideas about freedom and democracy, they were able to reach an agreement about the war and to work together.

Stalin and Churchill had four meetings. Stalin impressed Churchill by keeping even later hours than he did. Churchill reckoned his usual dinner hour was 1:30 A.M.! The two men didn't get along very well, but they did come to an agreement in the end. Churchill understood how bad things were in the Soviet Union. Despite the Soviets doing better in battle over the winter than had been expected, the Germans were gaining Soviet land and oil supplies. Stalin understood that the Second Front for 1942 would be in North Africa, not Europe. After another quick visit to Cairo, Churchill arrived in Britain at the end of August. That autumn, Allied forces made successful bombing raids on German cities, sending down thousands of tons of explosives.

On October 23, 1942, General Montgomery started the first real Allied attack on the Second Front from El-Alamein in Egypt. After twelve days of fighting, the British beat the Germans and Italians. This was a huge success. North Africa was secure, but the real success was the boost in morale the victory gave the Allied forces. The Allied forces finally felt like winners. Churchill gave another famous speech on November 10, "Now this is not the end. It is not even the beginning of the end. But it is, perhaps, the end of the beginning." On November 15, he ordered that all the church bells across England were to be rung to celebrate. From here onward, the Allies attacked instead of always defending.

In November 1942, the situation in the Soviet Union also improved. The Soviet troops finally began to defeat the Germans. By January 1943, their ultimate victory was certain, helped by the incredibly harsh Russian winter for which the Germans were unprepared.

Victory in Europe

Winston Churchill and Franklin Roosevelt met in Casablanca in Morocco in January 1943. They agreed that their enemies would have to surrender unconditionally and that no other terms would be accepted. After the meeting, Churchill took Roosevelt to Marrakech in Morocco for a visit and painted his only painting during the war years. Then he flew to Cairo, Turkey, Cyprus, and back to Cairo before traveling 2,000 miles (3,225 km) overland to Algiers. On February 12, a few days after returning to London, Churchill got sick with pneumonia. He never stopped working, but he could not do much during the thirty-one days it took him to recover.

This was the beginning of a busy year for Churchill. He was away a total of 172 days through January 1944. Still, he managed to keep the British and Allied war efforts well focused and moving forward. He traveled by boat, train, car, and airplane, all dangerous forms of transportation during war. He wrote, "These aeroplane journeys had to be taken as a matter of course during the war. None the less I always regarded them as dangerous excursions."

By the end of March, it was clear that the Allies safely held North Africa. Now they had to decide what to do next. Churchill wanted to invade Italy through Sicily and then capture Rome. On May 4, Churchill sailed for Washington, D.C., to meet with Roosevelt. He stayed in the White House once again and also visited Camp David (then called Shangri-La). Churchill also spoke to Congress during his fifteen-day stay. The victory in North Africa was made official on May 10, and he ordered that church bells be rung across England again. He wanted to celebrate the victory with the troops in Africa. On his way back, he flew to Gibraltar, Algiers, and Tunis. He went home on June 5.

At the beginning of July, the Germans launched their last attack on the Eastern Front. Now that its worst casualties were over, the Soviet Union was growing stronger. Stalin kept pushing for action in Europe. On July 9, British and U.S. forces invaded Sicily. The Italian leader, Mussolini, was dismissed on July 25. Allied forces gained control of Sicily on August 17. By September 7, Italy had made peace with the Allies. Germany quickly occupied northern Italy. There was heavy fighting in Italy for several more months.

Having fought alone for so long, Britain was now dwarfed by the size of its allies. Roosevelt and Stalin wanted to invade France as soon as possible in an operation called Overlord. It was scheduled for May 1944. Churchill had wished to regain a foothold in Europe since 1940, but he was cautious. He wanted to wait until August 1944 to invade. Meanwhile, he wanted to put more effort into the war in the Mediterranean.

Although they agreed on Overlord, Roosevelt and Stalin had never met in person. Churchill and Roosevelt were working closely together.

They even had a direct telephone line in the Cabinet War Rooms. It took a large roomful of coding equipment to scramble the signals to try to send them safely. The Germans could sometimes intercept the calls, so the two leaders were always cautious about what they said to each other. Churchill was by far the most mobile leader of the three. He sailed again to meet Roosevelt in Quebec on August 4. He brought about two hundred people with him on this trip, including Clementine and Mary. In Quebec, they agreed that a U.S. general would lead the Overlord forces in Europe. They also decided to have a meeting with Stalin in the autumn. Once again, they talked about how to handle the next steps in the war.

When Churchill got home on September 20, he faced another busy period. He went to address the House of Commons the next day. He spoke about his travels and responded to criticism that he was away too much by saying that he was doing vital business for the country.

TEHRAN CONFERENCE

On November 12, Churchill set off for another meeting with Roosevelt and Stalin, bringing Sarah and Randolph along for company. They flew to Algiers, Malta, and Cairo. Roosevelt met Churchill in Cairo and spent a few days discussing the war and visiting the pyramids and the Sphinx. The Tehran, Iran, conference was successful. Roosevelt and Stalin met in person for the first time, and all three leaders agreed on policies. They decided how to deal with the German-occupied lands after the war ended. They also worked out the fine points of Overlord. Roosevelt decided that General Dwight Eisenhower would lead the operation.

After the dinner party held to celebrate Churchill's sixty-ninth birthday, he said, "On my right sat the President of the United States, on my left the Master of Russia. Together we controlled a large preponderance of the naval and three-quarters of the air forces of the world, and could direct armies of nearly twenty millions of men. . . ."

On December 2, Churchill flew back to Cairo. He had more meetings with Roosevelt and other leaders in the area. Although he was not ill, Churchill was clearly worn out. He had frequent colds and upset stomachs. His colleagues and friends thought he looked exhausted. He flew to Tunis on December 10, and on December 11, he became very ill. Specialists flew in, and so did Clementine. By Christmas Eve, he had recovered enough from this latest bout with pneumonia and heart trouble to attend a meeting. After Christmas, he went to Marrakech to recover his strength. He returned to London on January 18, 1944.

Death Camps

Hitler and his government controlled by the Nazi Party put millions of people to death in camps located in German-held lands. No one knows exactly how many, but it was between six and thirteen million people. Many of the victims were Jews, but Polish Catholics, homosexuals, communists, Romany, and other people the Nazis hated were also imprisoned and killed.

Many citizens and politicians did their best to help refugees from German-held lands. In 1942, the Allied leaders denounced "this bestial policy of cold-blooded extermination." Still, most people were shocked by the horror of the camps as they were found at the end of the war. Winston Churchill and other leaders vowed to hunt down and bring the murderers responsible for the carnage to justice.

As soon as he landed, Churchill went to the House of Commons and answered questions, then lunched with the king and had a War Cabinet meeting. He started serious planning for Overlord, holding weekly meetings with key people, including General Eisenhower. He was in London when British and American troops made another attack on Italy at Anzio, 40 miles (65 km) south of Rome, on January 21. It took until May to clear the way to Rome.

People said Churchill was looking old and tired as he kept up his tough schedule. After giving a speech to the House of Commons in February, he told a friend, "it was a great effort . . . to make these speeches now." During a radio broadcast at the end of March, he sounded tired as well. He won another vote of confidence in the House of Commons. He had moments of energy but was worried about the Overlord invasion and about what the Soviet Union would do with Eastern Europe after the war. He still hated communism and thought the Soviet Union was trying to rule places such as Poland.

D-DAY

In the days before the Allied invasion, known as D-Day, Churchill brightened up and planned to go over for the landings himself. Eisenhower and Churchill's ministers were appalled. King George VI wanted to go, too, but he agreed to stay behind and talked Churchill into staying as well. The invasion on June 6 was a success. Although about 3,000 troops died that day, more than 150,000 landed safely. Six days later, Churchill went to France to see the battlegrounds for himself.

It took until August 25 for the Allies to reach Paris, but their progress was swift after that. They freed Brussels on September 3. While fighting in the north swept forward, plans for an invasion of the south of France were pushing ahead. Churchill was firmly against these plans, but the Americans were just as firmly in support of them. Churchill and Roosevelt argued over the decision. Churchill went to Italy from August 10 to 29 for meetings, including one with Pope Pius XII, and for some

In the D-Day invasion, Allied troops landed on the beaches of Normandy, France.

relaxation. He also watched the south of France landings from a ship while there. He considered this secondary French landing to be a diversion from Overlord and operations in northern Italy.

MEETINGS AROUND THE WORLD

Churchill traveled to Quebec again on September 4. He had a fever and pneumonia again but arrived in good spirits. Churchill assured Roosevelt that Britain would fight to end the war with Japan after the war in Europe was over. Before that happened, Churchill repeated his fears that the Soviet Union would take too strong a role in Europe's future if the American and British armies let the Soviet armies get to key cities first. Roosevelt felt that cooperation between the Soviets and the Americans would win the war and didn't want to sour this by arguing over Europe's political future. However, the two men had a good conference, and Churchill went home in a very good mood.

Although he only got back on September 26, Churchill left London again on October 7. This time, he went to Moscow to meet with Stalin. He was hoping to push the issue about the political future of Europe, especially in Greece and Poland. He had a productive meeting but suffered again from ill health. He wrote to King George VI, "At or after the very lengthy feasts, and very numerous cordial toasts, it has been possible to touch on many grave matters in an easy fashion." Churchill and Stalin agreed to the percentages of control they would have over important European states. Stalin later went back on some of their agreements, but he did leave Greece alone as he had promised. Churchill had less luck with Poland, where he wanted to create a cooperative government between the communists and democratic leaders. In the end, the Soviet Union gained control of Poland.

Returning to Europe, Churchill walked down the Champs Elysées in Paris with French general Charles de Gaulle. They celebrated French freedom with the cheering crowds. Churchill faced criticism from British and American newspapers because the war was still grinding on. Hitler held onto Germany and fought hard in Italy. A German counter-attack in France that December, the Battle of the Bulge, cost about eighty thousand American lives.

Churchill was worried about the fighting in Greece between the communist party and the king. He flew there on Christmas Day to hold a meeting with all the Greek leaders to try to restore peace and a democratic government. Soon after, Greece did manage to reach this end. Although Churchill was home for the New Year, he was back in France on January 3, 1945, to meet with General Eisenhower.

PROBLEMS AT HOME

Criticism from the press was nothing compared to the criticism Churchill faced at home from his colleagues. He was accused of running the government badly. They said he was away too often, didn't prepare for their meetings about British policy, and was not listening to the advice his expert advisors gave him. He weathered a political storm in January and then got ready to leave again. This time, he was off to Malta for a meeting with Roosevelt before another meeting with Roosevelt and Stalin in Yalta. His daughter Sarah came along.

Malta wasn't a success because Churchill was ill again. At Yalta, from February 5 to 11, Roosevelt was also weak and ill. The three leaders talked about how the United Nations would be formed and once again addressed the issue of control of Poland. Roosevelt made it clear that the "United States would take all reasonable steps to preserve peace, but not at the expense of keeping a large army indefinitely in Europe." This made Churchill feel even more strongly about the importance of creating a European alliance against communist forces. After the meeting, he went briefly to Athens again and was greeted by cheering crowds. Then he said good-bye to Roosevelt for the last time and went home via Cairo, landing in Britain on February 19. He always seemed revived by his meetings, even when they didn't achieve much.

Allied forces bombed many German cities that January, February, and March with shocking success. After the complete destruction of the city of Dresden, the bombing tailed off. Churchill went to join the

At Yalta, Churchill, Roosevelt, and Stalin (from left to right) met to discuss postwar Europe and the United Nations.

V Weapons

As the war neared its end, Hitler unleashed a new horror on Britain. From June through August 1944, about 2,500 V1 flying bombs fell. About six thousand people died from these "doodlebugs." In September, a new version, the V2 rocket, was sent and kept falling for 177 days. About 1,100 rockets killed 3,000 people. They frayed exhausted nerves even further.

Allied forces as they crossed the Rhine River into the heart of Germany at the end of March. On April 12, Roosevelt died suddenly. He missed the German surrender by weeks. Soon after his death, the Germans lost ground as the Allies took city after city. Mussolini was killed, and Hitler committed suicide. On May 7, the Germans surrendered unconditionally. Despite these great victories, Churchill wrote to Clementine, "I need scarcely tell you that beneath these triumphs lie poisonous politics and deadly international rivalries."

By the end of the war, the American forces in Europe numbered three million and the British one million. Winston Churchill had traveled 125,000 miles (201,168 km). He had spent 800 hours at sea and 350 hours in the air. He always had with him secretaries to take dictation and a traveling map room so he could keep track of the war. Churchill was still weak and often ill. He had to be carried up stairs and spent many days in bed. He did, however, make a great effort to join the festivities on Victory in Europe (VE) Day, May 8, 1945. The entire country took to the streets and celebrated. Churchill spoke to the nation and the House of Commons, met with his Cabinet and the king, and spoke to a crowd in Whitehall. He shouted, "This is your victory." They shouted back, "No, it is yours."

Churchill signs the victory symbol to the crowds outside Buckingham Palace on VE Day.

TEN

After the War

By the time the war in Europe ended, the Labour and Conservative coalition government was falling apart. Churchill wanted to keep it going until the war was over with Japan, but the Labour Party leaders decided it would be better to hold a general election as soon as possible. So, on May 23, Churchill dissolved the coalition and created a temporary government while campaigning started for the election.

At the beginning of June, Churchill gave the first of a series of campaign speeches. Each party was given a series of slots in which to broadcast speeches on the radio, which about half of the adults in the country listened to. The first speech was a disaster. Churchill, who had spent the war telling people to pull together, stand firm, and work together as a nation, suddenly went on a political attack. Awful death-camp scenes were fresh in people's minds, and Hitler's Gestapo police were thought to be one of the most evil forces in Nazi Germany. Therefore, Churchill's words were truly shocking when he said, "No Socialist government conducting the entire life and industry of the country could afford to allow free, sharp or violently worded expressions of public discontent. They would have to fall back on some kind of Gestapo, no doubt very humanely directed in the first instance."

In saying this, Churchill showed that he was out of touch with what British citizens now wanted. During the war, Britain had adopted a number of socialist policies to make things fairer and run smoothly while the nation's energy was focused on winning the war. Now people didn't want to return to strong class divisions and poor living and working conditions. They wanted a reward for all their efforts during the war. They didn't want an all-controlling government that would stamp out personal freedoms, but they did want a fairer homeland in which people shared the good things in life more equally. Even policies such as food and clothing rationing, which seemed harsh to those used to having plenty, gave those used to having nothing far more than they had before.

Clement Attlee, the leader of the Labour Party, replied to Churchill's speech.

When I listened to the Prime Minister's speech last night in which he gave such a travesty of the policy of the Labour Party, I realized at once what was his object. He wanted the electors to understand how great was the difference between Winston Churchill, the great leader in war of a united nation, and Mr. Churchill, the party Leader of the Conservatives. He feared that those who had accepted his leadership in war might be tempted out of gratitude to follow him further. I thank him for having disillusioned them so thoroughly.

Over the following weeks, Churchill campaigned with energy. Most people thought he would win in spite of his misunderstanding of public opinion. The election was held on July 5, but the votes weren't counted for another three weeks because the soldiers' votes had yet to reach England. After the election, Churchill went on a painting vacation. He then went to the next meeting of the three world leaders in Potsdam on July 15 with Stalin and the new U.S. president, Harry S. Truman. Attlee came along, too, in case he became the next prime minister. Not a lot was agreed on at the conference, but Truman and Churchill did agree to use the atom bomb on Japan there. Churchill and Attlee both went

Sarah's Letter

Churchill's daughter Sarah was working at an air base to the west of London when the political campaign started. She wrote a letter to her father on June 5, 1945, about his speech on the radio.

You see the people I know who are Labour, don't vote Labour for ideals or belief, but simply because life has been hard for them, often, an unequal struggle, and they think that only by voting Labour will their daily struggle become easier. . . . Because Socialism as practised in the war, did no one any harm, and quite a lot of people good. The children of this country have never been so well fed or healthy, what milk there was, was shared equally, the rich didn't die because their meat ration was no larger than the poor; and there is no doubt that the common sharing and feeling of sacrifice was one of the strongest bonds that unified us. So why, they say, cannot that common feeling of sacrifice be made to work as effectively in peace?

Churchill campaigned hard to regain the public's support, but his party did not receive enough votes to hold on to the prime minister's office.

home for the vote counting on July 25. By the next morning, it was clear that Labour had won about twice as many seats in Parliament as the Conservatives had, and Churchill was no longer prime minister.

Even though he was shocked and saddened by this news, Churchill acted strong. He went to the king to resign and then gave a statement to the public. He said,

> Immense responsibilities abroad and at home fall upon the new Government, and we must all hope that they will be successful in bearing them. It only remains for me to express to the British people, for whom I have acted in these perilous years, my profound gratitude for the unflinching, unswerving support which they have given me during my task. . .

LEADER OF THE OPPOSITION

After the Churchills moved out of 10 Downing Street, they stayed with family and in hotels until Chartwell and their new London house were ready to be lived in later that autumn. Overall, Churchill was a kinder man after the war, though right after the election, Clementine said, "He is so unhappy [and] that makes him very difficult."

Money was a concern again, and it looked as if the family might have to sell Chartwell. One of Churchill's friends and supporters, Lord Camrose, decided to raise money to buy Chartwell and then give it to the National Trust, an organization that keeps sites of national importance preserved for people to visit and enjoy. While Churchill was alive it would continue to serve as the family house, but after he died, the National Trust would open it to the public. This was Churchill's last financial crisis. By the end of 1946, Churchill had plenty of money again from his writings and the Chartwell sale. He started writing *The Second World War*, helped by a team of researchers. As before, his output was huge. The book grew into six volumes by the time it was done. When each volume was published, it sold an enormous number of copies.

Winston Churchill was now seventy-one. He was a firm leader of the Conservative Party in opposition to the Labour government. Although

Victory Over Japan

On August 6, 1945, the Allies dropped an atomic bomb on the Japanese city of Hiroshima. At the time, 138,690 people died. On August 9, the city of Nagasaki was destroyed by another atomic bomb, and 48,857 people died. Many more have died since then from radiation illnesses caused by the bombs. Allied leaders thought that the alternative was the death of a similar number of Allied and Japanese soldiers caused by an invasion of the Japanese islands. On August 15, 1945, Japan surrendered to the Allies, and World War II was over.

some of the M.P.s thought they would do better with a younger leader, most supported Churchill. He was usually in the House of Commons for important debates but was more often away. Most of his travels were vacations and painting trips, but he also went on lecture tours.

In 1946, Churchill went to the United States for three months and gave a famous speech in Fulton, Missouri. He said that an "iron curtain has descended" across Europe between the communist and democratic worlds. He said that the United States and Britain would have to work together to resist war with the Soviet Union. Newspapers in the United States, Britain, and the Soviet Union were unhappy with his speech. Stalin was critical. The speech was shocking at the time, but it accurately predicted what would happen during the Cold War. Churchill also supported the creation of a European union. It would be many years before a true union was created, but he helped the countries forge its beginnings.

Postwar Conditions

After the war ended, food shortages got worse instead of better. Suddenly, the countries that had food had to feed all the starving people they had liberated. It took years before everyone had enough food to eat and clothes to wear. All this work rebuilding Britain meant everyone had a job. In the early 1950s, Britain was the second-richest country in the world after the United States. But a reviving Europe quickly passed the British lead because of the strict government controls the Labour Party began after the war. Still, by the late 1950s, many British citizens owned refrigerators, televisions, washing machines, vacuum cleaners, and small cars.

He wanted Europe to work together for peace and economic wealth, and also to keep communism away.

In February 1947, Churchill's brother, Jack, died, which made Churchill very sad. Churchill's health went up and down. Sometimes he traveled for his health. He spent the winters in warm places to keep his bad colds and pneumonia to a minimum. He had a hernia operation and a stroke in 1949 that was kept secret.

PRIME MINISTER AGAIN

At the beginning of 1950, a general election was called. Hard campaigning and a greater understanding of the public's issues and needs gave the Conservative Party great gains. Labour won, but only had a majority of six seats instead of its nearly two hundred in 1945. Churchill pushed

President Harry S. Truman stands behind Churchill as he gives a speech at Westminister College in Fulton, Missouri. This speech caused quite a stir.

hard on the Labour government, thinking it would fall before long. He used speeches and other tactics, such as keeping the M.P.s sitting all night over and over, until everyone was worn out and grumpy.

Churchill celebrated his fiftieth anniversary as an M.P. on October 1, 1950. A year later, he started campaigning for the next general election. At the end of October 1951, the Conservatives won a majority of twenty-six seats over Labour, and Churchill was made prime minister again at the age of seventy-six.

After calling most of his old friends and advisors back into government, Churchill settled down into his familiar routine. He spent less and less time dealing with policy matters and was once again criticized for how he used his cabinet. He could be brilliant sometimes, but he was clearly older and more tired than he liked to admit. He loved to play a card game called bezique and spent more time playing it than he did reading the policy documents sent to him.

The United States, with its nuclear weapons, protected Western Europe from the Soviet Union. Churchill thought this was useful. However, he wanted to do something to make sure that nuclear bombs didn't end the world. He met with the U.S. president four times, in

Hallmark Cards

In the summer of 1950, Joyce C. Hall, the founder of Hallmark Cards, visited Winston Churchill at Chartwell. He decided to use eighteen of Churchill's paintings as Hallmark Christmas cards in 1950. After Churchill died, Hallmark printed Christmas cards for Clementine every year, using one of Churchill's paintings as the picture.

January 1952, January 1953, December 1953, and June 1954. When Eisenhower took over after Truman in 1953, Churchill was concerned that he didn't really understand how awful nuclear bombs could be.

In February 1952, King George VI died, and Princess Elizabeth became queen. Her coronation ceremony took place in May 1953. Churchill was saddened by the king's death. He loved the grandeur of the coronation but found all the ceremonies very tiring. In March 1953, Stalin died. Churchill was made a Knight of the Garter by Queen Elizabeth II. He was now called Sir Winston Churchill. In June, he had a severe stroke, which was kept secret. He recovered at Chartwell and

Churchill walks in the procession at the Garter Awards ceremony, during which he became a Knight of the Garter.

Chequers during the summer, but was increasingly ill and tired. He probably would have resigned then, but Anthony Eden, his deputy, was also ill and couldn't take over as prime minister. Churchill was well enough in the autumn to get back to business.

In October 1953, Churchill was honored with the Nobel Prize for Literature. On November 3, he gave a speech to the House of Commons in which he wondered whether "the advance of destructive weapons enables everyone to kill everybody else [so] nobody will want to kill anyone at all." While this was an optimistic idea, it gives a clue as to why he remained in government. He wanted to do what he could to limit the horror of nuclear weapons. In December, Churchill met with Eisenhower and French Prime Minister Laniel in Bermuda. The meeting wasn't a great success and did little to further Churchill's goal of getting

This photograph is one of the few images of Churchill's portrait by Graham Sutherland. Churchill hated the portrait, and later it was destroyed.

disarmament talks started between the Allies and the Soviet Union. Eisenhower said he thought the Soviet Union was an unchanged enemy and that nuclear weapons were now as acceptable to use as old-style bombs. In June 1954, Eisenhower appeared to reverse himself on the talks with the Soviet Union, and Churchill was delighted. However, Eisenhower quickly went back to his earlier position, and the Soviets gave mixed signals about their willingness to hold serious talks. Churchill's hopes for disarmament were ended.

On November 30, 1954, Winston Churchill turned eighty. Only a few prime ministers have lived to be eighty years old in office. The House of Commons had a celebration, and the M.P.s gave him a portrait painted by Graham Sutherland. Churchill hated the portrait, and Clementine later had it destroyed. Clementine and their children were torn as to whether Winston should resign. They wanted him to be happy, and he was most happy while in office. On the other hand, they wanted his public image to be kept sparkling, not dirtied by his increasing lack of ability to govern. In the end, Churchill gave his last major speech, about nuclear arms, at the beginning of March 1955. He then said he would resign in April, and Anthony Eden prepared to take over as prime minister.

ELEVEN

A Great Life Ends

On April 4, 1955, the Churchills held a grand dinner party at 10 Downing Street for the queen and about fifty other guests. After seeing Queen Elizabeth and Prince Philip into their car, Winston Churchill went to sleep for the last time in the Prime Minister's house. The next day, he formally resigned to the queen and then went to Chartwell. There, he spent most of his remaining time in England, enjoying his country home and entertaining his guests, including his children and grandchildren.

During the next four years, Churchill finished writing *A History of the English Speaking Peoples,* his last major book, which he had begun before the war. He gave speeches, although no more in Parliament. Conservative leaders asked for his opinion from time to time, but he was not an active M.P. Although Randolph had lost his fourth election to Parliament by this time, two of his sons-in-law were M.P.s. Churchill spent a lot of time out of the country, enjoying the warmth of the south of France. Clementine and he spent a lot of time apart as always, but they also enjoyed their time together. As well as staying in friends' villas and hotels, the Churchills enjoyed boat trips.

The Churchills took a trip to Cap d'Ail, Monaco, to celebrate their anniversary with their family. Son Randolph (far left) and granddaughter Arabella (far right) were among the relatives who joined Winston and Clementine.

The Churchills celebrated their fiftieth wedding anniversary in 1958. Their children gave them a book of paintings of golden roses and planted a golden rose walk at Chartwell. In 1959, Churchill again visited the White House and President Eisenhower. In October, Churchill stood for election for the House of Commons for the last time and won. Churchill College at the University of Cambridge founded in his name, now holds his letters and papers in the Churchill Archives Centre. By the end of 1959, Churchill gave up painting and spent much of his time reading novels.

In June 1962, Churchill fell from his bed while staying in a hotel in France and broke his hip. He was flown home to England to recover. After he mended, he still traveled a bit, but his energy was almost gone. When President Kennedy made him an honorary U.S. citizen in 1963, he was not well enough to go there himself to accept the honor. He was fairly deaf by this point and often used a wheelchair. Kennedy said about Churchill, "In the dark days and darker nights when England stood alone—and most men save Englishmen despaired of England's life—he mobilized the English language and sent it into battle. The incandescent quality of his words illuminated the courage of his countrymen." Those

A Productive Life

By the time he died, Winston Churchill had created about five hundred paintings. He had published about fifty books that had been translated into about two thousand editions around the world. He had also written more than one thousand newspaper and magazine articles. His collected speeches fill eight thick volumes. His works and essays were published in thirty-eight volumes.

famous words about mobilizing the English language were first said by the brilliant American radio reporter, Edward R. Murrow, recalling Churchill's wartime speeches.

On July 27, 1964, Winston Churchill went to the House of Commons for the last time. In October, he left Chartwell for the last time. He went to his house in London, where he celebrated his ninetieth birthday and Christmas. On January 10, Winston Churchill had a massive

Churchill remained active late in his life. A few months before his death, he met with a film producer who was working on a film based on Churchill's *My Early Life*.

stroke. He fell into a coma and died on January 24, the same day his father had died seventy years before. Clementine lived for another twelve years, dying in December 1977.

A STATE FUNERAL

Before he died, many great and long-standing friends visited Winston Churchill's sickbed. After his death, his coffin lay in state in Westminster Hall at Westminster Abbey for three days. A guard of soldiers stood around the clock. About 300,000 people filed past his coffin to pay their respects. Many thousands more watched the procession of Churchill's coffin to the funeral service in St. Paul's Cathedral. Millions watched the whole funeral on television around the world. British people had a day off work to mark the occasion. After the funeral the coffin went by boat to Waterloo train station, then by special train to a station near Blenheim Palace, where he was born. A short burial service was held in Bladon church. Then Winston Churchill's body was buried next to his parents and brother in the churchyard. The bells were rung for three hours to honor him.

It seems right that a man who had such an influence over so many lives was given these high state honors at the end of his life. In the first two days after he was buried, about eighty thousand people waited three hours in a mile-long line to walk past his grave. They wanted to pay their last respects in person—many because they felt he had saved their homeland during its most perilous times. His strength, determination, and optimism made him a great man. His flaws and weaknesses made him interesting and human. Winston Churchill lives on today in many people's opinion as the greatest prime minister Britain ever had.

Hundreds of people crowded the streets of London to say good-bye to a beloved leader.

Timeline

1874 Winston Leonard Spencer Churchill is born on November 30 at Blenheim Palace.

1880 Churchill's brother, Jack, is born.

1882–1884 Churchill goes to St George's School, Ascot.

1884–1888 Churchill goes to Misses Thompsons' School, Brighton.

1885 Clementine Hozier is born on April 1.

1886 Lord Randolph resigns from the government.

1888–1892 Churchill goes to Harrow, a school in London.

1893–1895 Churchill goes to Sandhurst.

1895 Churchill's father, Lord Randolph, dies. Elizabeth Everest dies. Churchill is made an officer with the 4th Hussars. He goes to Cuba as a journalist.

1896 Churchill goes to India as an officer.

1897 Churchill gives his first political speech. He goes to Indian North-West Frontier as a soldier and a journalist.

1898 Churchill's first book, *The Story of the Malakand Field Force,* is published. He goes to Egypt as a soldier.

1899 Churchill stands in his first election in Oldham and loses. He goes to South Africa as a journalist. He is captured by the Boers and makes a famous escape. He publishes *The River War.*

1900 Churchill is elected as Conservative M.P. for Oldham. He publishes *Savrola, London to Ladysmith,* and *Ian Hamilton's March.*

1901 Churchill gives his first speech in the House of Commons.

1904 Churchill moves to the Liberal Party.

1905 Churchill is given his first government position, under-secretary of state at the Colonial Office.

1906 Churchill is elected as Liberal M.P. for Manchester. He publishes *Lord Randolph Churchill*.

1908 Churchill is given a new government job, president of the Board of Trade. He is defeated at Manchester, then elected at Dundee. He marries Clementine Hozier on September 12.

1909 Churchill's daughter Diana is born.

1910 Churchill is reelected at Dundee twice. He is made home secretary.

1911 Churchill's son, Randolph, is born. He is made First Lord of the Admiralty.

1913 Churchill takes flying lessons.

1914 Churchill gives up flying. His daughter Sarah is born.

World War I begins.

1915 Churchill is made chancellor of the Duchy of Lancaster. He resigns from the government in November. He starts painting. He joins the war in the trenches in Belgium.

Dardanelles campaign begins.

1916 Churchill returns to Parliament.

1917 Churchill is made minister of munitions. He is reelected in Dundee. He buys Lullenden in Sussex.

1918 Churchill is made secretary of state for war and air. His daughter Marigold is born.

World War I ends.

1919 Churchill briefly takes flying lessons again.

1921 Churchill is made secretary of state for the colonies. His mother and daughter Marigold die. He starts writing *The World Crisis*.

1922 Churchill buys Chartwell in Kent. His daughter Mary is born. He loses the election in Dundee.

1923 Churchill loses the election in West Leicester.

1924 Churchill loses the election in Westminster. He wins with Conservative backing in Epping. He is made Chancellor of the Exchequer and becomes a Conservative again.

1926 Churchill publishes a government newspaper.

The General Strike takes place.

1929 Churchill is reelected in Epping, but the Conservative government is out of power so he loses his government job.

1930 Churchill publishes *My Early Life* and works on projects at Chartwell. He is made chancellor of Bristol University.

1931 Churchill is hit by a car in New York City and is badly hurt. He is reelected in Epping.

1935 Churchill is reelected in Epping.

1938 Churchill continues to oppose appeasement and warns of the danger from Germany. He starts writing *The History of the English Speaking Peoples*.

1939 Churchill is made First Lord of the Admiralty.

World War II begins. Britain enters the war.

1940–1941 The Blitz takes place.

1940 Churchill becomes prime minister.

France falls to Germany. Troops are evacuated from Dunkirk. The Battle of Britain takes place.

1941 Churchill meets Franklin D. Roosevelt at Placentia Bay. He meets Roosevelt in Washington, D.C. He has a mild heart attack.

Germany attacks the Soviet Union. Japan attacks Pearl Harbor. The United States enters World War II.

1942 Churchill meets Roosevelt in Washington, D.C. He wins two votes of confidence and meets Stalin in Moscow.

Allies are victorious at El-Alamein.

1943 Churchill meets Roosevelt in Casablanca, Washington, D.C., Quebec, and Cairo. He visits troops in North Africa. He meets with Roosevelt and Stalin in Teheran.

Allies achieve peace with Italy.

1944 Churchill meets with Roosevelt in Quebec. He meets with Stalin in Moscow.

The D-Day landings occur. Paris is freed by the Allies. Germany fires V1 and V2 rockets at Britain.

1945 Churchill meets Roosevelt in Malta and then Roosevelt and Stalin in Yalta. He meets with Truman and Stalin in Potsdam. He is elected in Woodford Green but resigns as prime minister.

U.S. president Roosevelt dies. Germany surrenders. Victory in Europe (VE) is declared on May 8. A general election is called in Britain. Atom bombs devastate Hiroshima and Nagasaki in Japan. Japan surrenders.

1946 Churchill begins writing *The Second World War*. He sells Chartwell to friends, but lives there for the rest of his life.

1947 Churchill's brother Jack dies.

1949 Churchill has a stroke.

1950 Churchill is reelected in Woodford. He celebrates fifty years in Parliament.

1951 Churchill is reelected in Woodford. Conservatives win, and he becomes prime minister again.

1952 Churchill meets with Truman in Washington, D.C.

King George VI dies. Queen Elizabeth takes the crown.

1953 Churchill meets with Dwight D. Eisenhower in Washington, D.C., and Bermuda. He has a severe stroke. He wins the Nobel Prize for Literature. He is knighted Sir Winston Churchill.

Stalin dies.

1955 Churchill is reelected in Woodford. He gives his last major speech in Parliament. He resigns as prime minister.

1956–1962 Churchill's health worsens.

1958 Churchill celebrates his fiftieth wedding anniversary with Clementine.

1959 Churchill is reelected in Woodford. He visits Eisenhower in Washington, D.C.

1962 Churchill breaks his hip in France.

1963 President John Kennedy gives Churchill honorary U.S. citizenship.

1964 Churchill leaves the House of Commons for the last time in June.

1965 Churchill has a massive stroke on January 10. He dies on January 24.

To Find Out More

BOOKS

Ashworth, Leon, *Winston Churchill*. Evans Brothers, 2002.

Reynoldson, Fiona, *Winston Churchill*. Chicago: Heinemann Library, 2001.

Severance, John B. *Winston Churchill: Soldier, Statesman, Artist*. Clarion Books, 1996.

ORGANIZATIONS AND ONLINE SITES

The Churchill Centre
1150 17th Street NW, Suite 307
Washington, DC 20036
http://www.winstonchurchill.org

The organization's Web site has a comprehensive collection of information, scholarly articles, student activities, and events concerning Winston Churchill, together with samples of his speeches.

Churchill College, Cambridge
http://www.chu.cam.ac.uk/archives/

The college holds Winston Churchill's papers and archives, as well as those of other important people of his time.

The Churchill Society
http://www.churchill-society-london.org.uk

This site is a vast biographical resource, with detailed information on Churchill's life and award-winning "school pages."

First World War
http://www.firstworldwar.com

This site has an excellent summary of the events, causes, and aftermath of World War I.

Time Magazine
http://www.time.com/time/time100/leaders/profile/churchill.html

Time magazine's top 100 people of the twentieth century includes a profile of Winston Churchill and recorded speeches.

A Note on Sources

There are so many books, videos, audio recordings, and photographs about Winston Churchill that the sheer amount of information can be bewildering. However, as you get more interested in his life and the fascinating times during which he lived, all this information means you have plenty to dig into. I would recommend reading his book about World War II, *The Second World War.* He made a short version of the six-volume work, which is still long at nearly a thousand pages. However, it really shows how he saw things and is full of interesting stories. Check out your library for videos and DVDs about him. Some movies have been made to tell stories about his life, the best of which are *Churchill: The Wilderness Years,* starring Robert Hardy, and *Churchill,* a documentary narrated by his official biographer, Sir Martin Gilbert. There are also collections of his speeches and official visits captured on black-and-white movie news film. Hearing Churchill speak is always moving. Listen to his speeches if you can. There are recordings on many of the Web sites about him. Nothing brings you closer to Churchill's power than hearing him deliver those momentous words.

—*Tristan Boyer Binns*

Index

About the Author

Tristan Boyer Binns has an English degree from Tufts University. She has written twenty-five books for children and young adults on subjects from the American flag to Fort Laramie to the CIA. She has taught creative writing to children and adults and has conducted writing workshops. Before beginning her writing career, Tristan was publishing director for an international library-book publisher. Researching people's lives and the history of daily life is a real joy for her.